Master Time Co v. De Jongh U.S. Supreme Court Transcript of Record with Supporting Pleadings

WARREN H YOUNG, BRUCE MACGIBBON

Master Time Co v. De Jongh

Petition / WARREN H YOUNG / 1967 / 1082 / 390 U.S. 1041 / 88 S.Ct. 1633 / 20 L.Ed.2d 303 / 2-5-1968

Master Time Co v. De Jongh

Brief in Opposition (P) / BRUCE MACGIBBON / 1967 / 1082 / 390 U.S. 1041 / 88 S.Ct. 1633 / 20 L.Ed.2d 303 / 4-15-1968

Master Time Co v. De Jongh U.S. Supreme Court Transcript of Record with Supporting Pleadings

Table of Contents

IN THE

Supreme Court of the United States

OCTOBER TERM, 1967

No. 1082 *689*

IN THE MATTER OF MASTER TIME COMPANY, LTD. a
Virgin Islands Corporation, *Petitioner,*

v.

THE HONORABLE PERCY deJONGH, ETC., *Respondent.*

PETITION FOR A WRIT OF CERTIORARI TO THE UNITED STATES COURT OF APPEALS FOR THE THIRD CIRCUIT

WARREN H. YOUNG
46 King Street
Christiansted, St. Croix
U. S. Virgin Islands 00820

JAMES H. ISHERWOOD
46 King Street
Christiansted, St. Croix
U. S. Virgin Islands 00820

Attorneys for Petitioner

Of Counsel:

YOUNG AND ISHERWOOD
U. S. Virgin Islands

PRESS OF BYRON S. ADAMS PRINTING, INC., WASHINGTON, D. C.

INDEX

INDEX OF CITATIONS

IN THE

Supreme Court of the United States

OCTOBER TERM, 1967

———

No.

———

IN THE MATTER OF MASTER TIME COMPANY, LTD. a
Virgin Islands Corporation, *Petitioner,*

v.

THE HONORABLE PERCY DEJONGH, ETC., *Respondent.*

———

PETITIONS FOR A WRIT OF CERTIORARI TO REVIEW THE JUDGMENT OF THE UNITED STATES COURT OF APPEALS FOR THE THIRD CIRCUIT ENTERED IN THE CASE ON SEPTEMBER 29, 1967

———

OPINIONS BELOW

The memorandum opinion of the District Court of the Virgin Islands in this case (App. A at pp. 1a-2a) (unreported) refers to previous opinions in related cases brought by Virgo Corporation against the Government of the Virgin Islands the first of March 14,

1966 (App. C at pp. 4a-15a), and the second of June 2, 1966 (App. D at pp. 16a-34a) *Virgo Corporation* v. *Ralph M. Paiewonsky*, 254 F. Suppl. 405 (1966). The citation of the Court of Appeals Opinion (App. E at pp. 35a-63a) is not as yet available to Petitioner.

JURISDICTION

The judgment of the Court of Appeals was entered on September 29, 1967. A timely petition for rehearing was filed on October 23, 1967 and was denied on November 7, 1967. The jurisdiction of this Court is invoked under 28 U.S.C. § 1254.

QUESTIONS PRESENTED

Whether the legislative powers of the Virgin Islands as limited by § 36 of the 1936 Organic Act, providing that no new export duties shall be levied except by the Congress, and the 1954 Organic Act extending the legislative powers of the Virgin Islands to all rightful subjects of legislation permit the passage of a discriminatory tax designed to limit the export of locally manufactured goods to the United States.

STATUTES INVOLVED

Act of Congress dated June 22, 1936, PL 749, Ch. 699 § 36, 49 Stat. 1816, the pertinent portion of which is set out in full in Appendix H at p. 66a.

Act of Congress dated July 22, 1954, PL 558, Ch. 558, 68 Stat. 497, the pertinent portion of which is set out in full in Appendix L at pp. 92a-94a.

Act of Congress dated August 28, 1958, PL 85-851, 72 Stat. 1094, which is set out in full in Appendix I at pp. 67a-69a.

Act No. 1631 Sixth Legislature of the Virgin Islands of the United States 1966. Session Laws of the Virgin Islands 1966 p. 98, which is set out in full in Appendix K at pp. 76a-81a.

Act No. 1518 of the Sixth Legislature of the Virgin Islands of the United States 1965. Session Laws of the Virgin Islands 1965, Part 1, page 470, which is set out in full in Appendix J at pp. 70a-75a.

STATEMENT OF THE CASE

Favorable tariff treatment of goods manufactured in the Virgin Islands has resulted in the establishment of a number of Watch Factories there. More than 97% of such production is exported to the United States customs area.

On May 3, 1965, the Governor of the Virgin Islands appointed a special committee to study problems relating to the growth of this industry and to recommend legislation. The committee, on August 9, 1965, recommended the establishment of a quota system and a tax of $2.50 on each unit in excess of the quota. $2.50 is equivalent to the duty paid by foreign manufacturers on popular-sized watches. On August 25, 1965, the Legislature of the Virgin Islands enacted Act No. 1518 which was approved by the Governor. The Act authorized the Governor to set up quotas for the various manufacturers and impose a tax of $2.50 per watch allowing a credit of $2.47 for watches sold to U. S. Customers in accordance with the quota or sold outside of the U. S. Customs area. There appears to be no dispute that the purpose of the Act intended by the Legislature was to limit shipments to the United States.

The petitioner instituted suit to have the act declared void on the grounds that the Government of the Virgin

Islands had no power to levy export duties. The District Court of the Virgin Islands, on motion for summary judgment held in favor of Petitioner on March 16, 1966.

On the day the Judgment of the District Court was entered the Legislature passed Act No. 1631 which modified the previous Act by classifying the tax as a production tax of $2.47 for all watches produced in excess of such quota.

Petitioner challenged the new law and on June 21, 1966, Judgment was once more entered for Petitioner and the District Courts decision was appealed to the Third Circuit Court of Appeals which held that the tax was a production tax and not an export duty, and that the 1954 Organic Act had as a matter of statutory construction repealed the provision of § 36 of the 1936 Act limiting the right to levy export duties. It ordered the case remanded with instructions to dismiss the complaint.

This is one of two cases having substantially similar facts decided at the same time by the Third Circuit.

REASONS FOR GRANTING THE WRIT

I. The Circuit Court Erred in Finding Act No. 1631 Was a Local Production Tax and Not an Export Duty.

The Court in finding that "the controlling fact is that the taxes attached while the watches were in process of their manufacture and before their sale and possible export" has ignored the fact that Section (a) of Act 1631 provides that the tax shall be imposed when the goods are sold or *removed* for sale, consumption or use. The word "removed" standing alone and unexplained would in its normal use mean removed from the Virgin Islands, or export.

Despite this clear language the Circuit Court found such tax an excise tax levied upon the production of watches in the Virgin Islands rather than a tax on goods entering commerce. It used as an example *Canton Railroad Co.* v. *Rogan,* 340 U.S. 511, 71 S.Ct. 447 (1951), which permitted the nondiscriminatory taxation of gross receipts of a company supplying Port services performed wholly within a state but whose business related to goods intended for export. It did not explain *A. G. Spaulding Bros.* v. *Edwards,* 262 U.S. 66; 43 S.Ct. 485 (1923), and *Richfield Oil Corp.* v. *State Board of Equalization,* 329 U.S. 69; 67 S.Ct. 156 (1946), which clearly refer to the goods themselves holding that such sale or removal is a portion of the export process. In the *Spaulding* case it was held that the sale of the goods is the act that commits the goods for export and that their removal to the ship is clearly export.

Thus the Government of the Virgin Islands affixes its tax at the very point where the goods enter the export trade and the Circuit Court in finding otherwise is interpreting a statute contrary to the precedents of this Court.

The fact that the Virgin Islands tax discriminates against goods intended for the U. S. market by imposing an additional $2.47 tax on those goods entering the stream of commerce in excess of the quota further illustrates the intention of the local legislature not to tax "*manufacture*" but to tax and limit "*commerce*" in such goods.

In § 3(a) the Act provides that in setting up the quota allotment, the Governor shall determine after due investigation the total annual consumption of watches of all kinds within the Customs Area of the United States, and shall allocate among manufacturers of watches in the Virgin Islands 1/9 of such annual consumption.

§ 6 provides that the Governor in the apportionment of quotas may take into account the production of watches and other timing devices by the same company or affiliates in any other territory or possession of the United States.

These Sections reinforced by the Amendment of Act 1518 by Act 1631 in an attempt to change the tax from an export duty to a production tax amply demonstrate the clear purpose of the legislature.

This purpose is recognized in the Opinion of the Circuit Court:

> "It is certainly true that the legislature had this possibility in mind in enacting the statute. The record is abundantly clear as to this."
>
> (Opinion Maris J. p. 19)

There is therefore no dispute that the clear and announced intention of the legislature is to restrict exports to the United States. Throughout the entire record including the Opinion of the Circuit Court no other purpose is even suggested.

By applying an almost confiscatory increase in the tax rate to the watches at the time that they would enter the stream of commerce, the Virgin Islands Legislature did not intend to achieve a local tax result, such as raising revenue. To the contrary, by the very increase in the rate, it has made further trade in the product manifestly unprofitable. Even if the tax could be called an "excise tax", the amount of the discriminatory increase (from 3¢ to $2.47) and the circumstances and history of its imposition show that it is intended as a measure to discourage or bar exports and commerce beyond an alloted amount.

II. The Circuit Court Acted Contrary to the Holdings of the Supreme Court in Decreeing That It Had No Authority to Consider the Substance Rather Than the Form of a Territorial Taxing Scheme.

Virtually all watches manufactured in the Virgin Islands are sold for delivery in the United States. The approximate U.S. duty on a foreign-made watch is $2.50 but watches manufactured in the Virgin Islands enter duty free. There is no quarrel with the right or power of the Virgin Islands Legislature to levy a production tax on watches and a 3¢ tax applicable to all watches would undoubtedly be considered such a tax, but a graduated tax moving immediately to $2.47 can only be considered such a tax if the Court closes its eyes completely to all of the surrounding facts and circumstances and relies entirely upon form rather than substance.

The Legislative history of the Act is so obviously directed to this end that the resulting limitation of commerce is not incidental to the taxing power but is the only direct, calculated, announced and accomplished purpose of the Act. To ignore this fact is to abandon completely the historic principles of judicial review of legislative actions. By whatever name it is called the tax here imposed is intended to and does unreasonably limit commerce between the territory and the United States.

This Court has announced its position in *American Oil Company* v. *Neill*, 380 U.S. 451, 85 S. Ct. 1130

(1965), "that when passing on the constitutionality of a state taxing scheme it is firmly established that this Court concerns itself with the practical operation of the tax, that is, substance, rather than form.

In *Connecticut General Life Ins. Co. v. Johnson,* 303 U.S. 77, 58 S. Ct. 436 (1938), this Court in interpreting the 14th Amendment denied a state the power to tax an economic benefit outside the state even though it had granted the subject corporation powers within the state. In the instant case the Virgin Islands Legislature seized upon the element of manufacture within its boundaries as a lever to limit by taxation the number of watches any manufacturer and its affiliates in other territories could ship to the United States. "In whatever language a statute may be framed its purpose must be determined by its natural and reasonable effect". *Henderson v. Mayor of New York,* 92 U.S. 259, 268, 23 L. Ed. 543; *Lawrence v. State Tax Commission,* 286 U.S. 276; 52 S. Ct. 556, 557; *State of Wisconsin v. J. C. Penney Co.,* 311 U.S. 435, 443, 61 S. Ct. 246.

Such illegal action could not be made legal simply because it called the tax a production tax rather than an export duty.

III. The Decision of the Circuit Court Is Contrary to the Ruling of This Court in Granville-Smith v. Granville-Smith.

In *Granville-Smith v. Granville-Smith,* 349 U.S. 1, 75 S. Ct. 553 (1955), both majority and minority opinions of this Court recognized the intention of Congress to permit the legislature to act upon matters of purely local concern and the rule of "rightful subjects of legislation" was applied by the majority and recognized by the minority. The very use of the word "rightful" indicates that judicial determination may be necessary.

The Circuit Court refused to apply this principle and decided the case on a narrow definition of whether the tax was or was not an excise tax rather than taking the broader and proper position that it is the subject matter of the legislation rather than the type of tax which should be considered by a reviewing Court. In Acts 1518 and 1631 the Virgin Islands Legislature sought to limit commerce between the territory and the various states of the United States, a matter of greater scope than the limitations upon the judiciary prescribed by the divorce statute involved in the *Granville-Smith* case.

The Court also erred in finding that the specific prohibition of Section 36 of the 1936 Organic Act against the levying of export duties had been repealed even though the same Congressional Committee Reports cited by the Court show a careful consideration of the limitations of such Section.

Judge Albert B. Maris, the writer of the Court's Opinion below, called attention to the Congressional Committee drafting the 1954 Organic Act to what he referred to as "an inadvertent omission" of a Section 37 repealing the 1936 Organic Act referring to confusion caused by such omission. Despite this letter Congress chose not to repeal the 1936 Act, this can hardly be called "inadvertence" a second time. Nor does it appear that Congress has considered the 1936 Act repealed, for the Virgin Islands Customs are still administered by the Treasury Department under authority of the same Section 36.

The 1954 Revised Organic Act as amended, must be held to repeal all inconsistent prior acts. An important question before the Court is whether the limitation on the power to impose new export duties is inconsistent with the legislative power granted in the Organic Act. This Act, amended subsequent to the *Granville-Smith* case, provides at 48 U.S.C. § 1574, that such power extends to "all rightful subjects of legislation not inconsistent with this Chapter . . ." The two important questions of whether Congress considered the imposition of export duties to be one of the limitations imposed by the Chapter and whether legislation affecting exports is a rightful subject of legislation remain unresolved and it is submitted that the Court below erred in answering both of them.

The Circuit Court should not have decided that a general legislative power repealed a previous specific limitation on that power.

Should it be that the legislature of the Virgin Islands may now impose export duties, the fact remains that it may do so only with respect to *"rightful subjects"* of legislation. The avowed purpose of this legislation is the control of commerce. Is this a rightful subject of territorial legislation?

The Constitution of the United States provides at Article I, § 8, no tax or duty may be laid on articles exported from any state. This is a limitation on the power of Congress itself. Can it be said that Congress, lacking such power, can confer this power upon a territorial legislature? If indeed it may, can such power be granted by the inclusion of a blanket authority under the wording "rightful subjects of legislation"?

CONCLUSION

The questions involved in this case concern the fundamental legislative power of the Government of the Virgin Islands and are of the greatest importance to this developing area. It is submitted that they are of such importance to the future of the Virgin Islands as to warrant this Court's attention and guidance.

Respectfully submitted,

WARREN H. YOUNG
46 King Street
Christiansted, St. Croix
U. S. Virgin Islands   00820

JAMES H. ISHERWOOD
46 King Street
Christiansted, St. Croix
U. S. Virgin Islands   00820

Attorneys for Petitioner

Of Counsel:

YOUNG AND ISHERWOOD
U. S. Virgin Islands

APPENDIX

APPENDIX A

IN THE DISTRICT COURT OF THE VIRGIN ISLANDS
DIVISION OF ST. CROIX

CIVIL No. 142—1965

MASTER TIME COMPANY, LTD., a Virgin Islands Corporation,
Plaintiff

v.

THE HONORABLE PERCY DEJONGH, as Commissioner of the Department of Finance of the Government of the Virgin Islands, *Defendant*

Memorandum Opinion

On October 4, 1965 the plaintiff filed its complaint seeking a judgment invalidating §§ 511 to 518 of Title 33 of the Virgin Islands Code as enacted by Act 1518. The defendant's answer denied that plaintiff's activities were in interstate or foreign commerce and alleging that the complaint failed to state a claim upon which relief can be granted and alleging that the Court lacks jurisdiction because the plaintiff has no standing to sue. On March 17, 1966 plaintiff filed a motion for judgment on the pleadings and defendant opposed said motion upon the pleadings by filing its motion in opposition on March 24, 1966. The basis of defendant's argument was the Virgin Islands Government by Act 1631 had amended the sections of law in issue and as amended the tax was alleged to no longer tax exports. Defendant stated in its moving papers that because of the changed circumstances the decision in Civil No. 165-1965 was no longer applicable. On June 13, 1966 plaintiff moved the Court for judgment on the pleadings. Both counsel were heard at that time and stipulated to submit the matter without oral argument. The matter was taken under advisement.

I

The primary issue originally raised was the validity of §§ 511 to 518 of Title 33 of the Virgin Islands Code as enacted by Act 1518. This Court adjudged said sections invalid in its decision of March 16, 1966 in Case No. 165-1965. Immediately thereafter Act No. 1631 was enacted amending the above sections. On June 2, 1966 in case No. 37-1966 this Court adjudged the amended sections enacted by Act No. 1631 to be invalid.

The Court finds in favor of the plaintiff upon its pleadings that §§ 511 to 518 of Title 33 of the Virgin Islands Code as enacted by Act 1518 and that §§ 511 to 518 of Title 33 of the Virgin Islands Code as amended by Act 1631 are invalid. The basis for the above decision is set forth extensively in this Court's Memorandum Opinion of March 14, 1966 in this Court's case No. 165-1965 and in this Court's Memorandum Opinion of June 2, 1966 in this Court's case No. 37-1966 and is therefore not reiterated here.

June 21, 1966

/s/ WALTER A. GORDON
Walter A. Gordon
Judge of the District Court

APPENDIX B

Order—June 24, 1966—Master Time

ORDER

The plaintiff's motion for judgment upon the pleadings having come on for hearing on June 13, 1966; the plaintiff appearing by its attorneys, Young, Isherwood and Marsh, Ronald H. Tonkin of counsel; and the defendant appearing by the Attorney General, Francisco Corneiro; and both counsel having been heard at that time; and having stipulated to submit the motion without oral argument; and the motion having been taken under advisement on June 13, 1966; and the Court having rendered its Memorandum Opinion on June 21, 1966; it is

HEREBY ORDERED that judgment be entered in favor of the plaintiff against the defendant invalidating §§ 511 to 518 of Title 33 of the Virgin Islands Code as enacted by Act 1518 and §§ 511 to 518 of Title 33 of the Virgin Islands Code as amended as enacted by Act 1631; it is

FURTHER ORDERED that each party shall bear their own costs.

June 24th, 1966

WALTER A. GORDON
Walter A. Gordon
Judge of the District Court

APPENDIX C

CIVIL No. 165—1965

VIRGO CORPORATION, A Virgin Islands Corporation,
Plaintiff

v.

RALPH M. PAIEWONSKY, Governor of the Virgin
Islands, et al., *Defendants*

Attorneys for the Plaintiff:

Howrey, Simon, Baker & Murchison
1707 H Street, Northwest
Washington, D.C.   20006

William Simon, Esq., of counsel
J. Coleman Bean, Esq., of counsel

Russel B. Johnson, Esq.
St. Croix, Virgin Islands

Attorney for the Defendant:

Attorney General of the Virgin Islands
Francisco Corneiro, Esq.
St. Thomas, Virgin Islands

Memorandum Opinion

On February 15, 1966, the plaintiff in the above entitled civil action brought on for hearing a motion for summary judgment and a motion for a preliminary injunction. The arguments on the above motions consumed the whole day and at the conclusion of the hearing the Court took the motions under advisement. Because of the serious questions raised, the Court deems it necessary to set forth its opinion in detail.

The plaintiff, a Virgin Islands corporation, filed the above entitled civil action in this Court against the defendants on November 18, 1965. The nature of the complaint was for a declaratory judgment and an injunction. The complaint was brought in two counts. In the first count of the complaint the plaintiff challenges the validity, legality and constitutionality of Title 33 Virgin Islands Code §§ 511-518 which is commonly known as the Watch Production Quota Act. In the second count of the complaint the plaintiff challenges the administration by the Virgin Islands Industrial Incentive Board and the Governor of the Virgin Islands of the tax exemption and subsidy provisions of Title 33 Virgin Islands Code § 4001 et seq. The Court will discuss each count separately in order not to confuse the facts and the law with respect to the pending motions.

With respect to the motion for summary judgment as to count one of the complaint in which the plaintiff challenges the Watch Production Quota Act, the plaintiff made the following contentions:

4

1. The Act is a burden on interstate commerce and is thus unconstitutional.

2. The Virgin Islands Legislature only has authority to enact legislation which is authorized by the Organic Act of the Virgin Islands. The Legislature had no authority to enact the Watch Production Quota Act because the Act was in contravention of the Organic Act of the Virgin Islands of the United States. [48 U.S.C.A. 1406i]

3. The Act unfairly discriminates between competitors and thus is in violation of the due process clause of the Constitution of the United States.

4. Assuming the constitutionality of the Act, the Act has been administered arbitrarily by the Governor.

5. Reserve allocations granted by the Governor were as a result of improper influence.

The defendants in opposition to the motion contended:

1. The Virgin Islands Legislature was acting within its province in enacting the Watch Production Quota Act.

2. The Court should not question the economic judgment of the Legislature.

3. Because the Virgin Islands is an unincorporated territory which has its own Bill of Rights, the Constitution of the United States is not applicable to the Virgin Islands.

4. The tax imposed by the Act is local and therefore does not hinder interstate commerce.

The following are the material uncontroverted facts with regard to count one of the complaint:

The plaintiff is a Virgin Islands corporation with its principal place of business at Frederiksted, St. Croix, Virgin Islands. Plaintiff manufactures watches in the Virgin Islands and sells those same watches in interstate and foreign commerce. Plaintiff is a wholly owned subsidiary of Timex, Limited, a Bermuda company, and is affiliated with and sells its entire production of watches to United States Time Corporation, a Connecticut corporation.

⋅ Plaintiff commenced its watch manufacturing in St. Croix in June, 1963 with a capital investment in excess of $300,000. It employs approximately 32 people with an annual income of approximately $100,000.

In August, 1965 the Legislature of the Virgin Islands in special session enacted bill number 2638 which added sections 511 to 518 to Title 33 Virgin Islands Code. The Governor of the Virgin Islands on August 30, 1965 approved this bill and it became effective as Act No. 1518. The provisions of this Act relevant to this controversy are:

a. Section 511 imposes a tax of $2.50 on each watch manufactured in the Virgin Islands for sale or use in the customs area of the United States. This section further provides that if the number of watches sold in the United States does not exceed the quota allocated to the manufacturer, then the tax shall be 3¢ instead of $2.50 per watch. On all other watches manufactured and sold, either in the Virgin Islands or outside the customs area of the United States, the tax is only 3¢ per watch.

b. Section 512 establishes a quota of 1,800,000 watches to be manufactured in the Virgin Islands *for export to the customs area of the United States* during the six-month period from October 1, 1965 to March 31, 1966.

c. Section 513 provides that for each twelve-month period subsequent to March 31, 1966, *the Governor shall allocate among the watch manufacturers in accordance with the formula provisions of Section 514(b) "such number of units as shall total 1/9 of annual consumption" in the customs area of the United States.* The section further provides that, of the total units to be allocated, five percent "shall be reserved as a quantity to supplement quotas allocated to manufacturers and to relieve against severe financial hardship, in accordance with the provisions of Section 515." (Emphasis supplied)

The history of this enactment would be most helpful in visualizing what will follow.

Under Paragraph (a) of General Headnote 3 of the Tariff Schedules of the United States [19 U.S.C.A. § 1202] articles produced in insular possessions, which includes the Virgin Islands, may enter the United States duty free if the articles do not contain foreign materials to the value of more than 50 percent of their total value. This tariff concession was made by Congress to help encourage economic development in the insular possessions and territories of the United States.

In the last five to six years, the watch assembly industry has developed rapidly in the Virgin Islands as a result of the tariff concessions which permit the assembled watches to enter the United States duty free. In 1964 approximately 9 percent or 2,400,000 watch movements consumed in the United States were assembled by eleven watch manufacturers in the Virgin Islands.

Because of the so-called flood of watches from the Virgin Islands to the United States, manufacturers of watches in the United States were lobbying in Congress to amend the tariff laws to stop Virgin Islands-made watches from entering the United States duty free.

In order to head off any action by the Congress, the Legislature of the Virgin Islands on June 25, 1964 passed Resolution Number 293 which stated:

"WHEREAS the continued ability of this industry to contribute to the economy of the Virgin Islands is partly dependent on the structure of the United States tariff laws with regard to the entry of watches and related products from the Virgin Islands and from foreign countries; and

*   *   *   *   *

WHEREAS the Legislature of the Virgin Islands is anxious to preserve for the people of the Virgin Islands and those who have invested substantial amounts in its economy the benefits of the watch manufacturing industry without inflicting undue injury on mainland manufacturers and their employees; Now, Therefore, be it

RESOLVED by the Legislature of the Virgin Islands:

SECTION 1. That it is the intention of the Legislature of the Virgin Islands to take such steps as may be necessary to alleviate the conditions that have led mainland manufacturers to request congressional action including the imposition of production taxes of the sort now imposed on the woolen textile industry by Section 501-508 of Title 33 of the Virgin Islands Code on the manufacture of clocks, watches, and watch movements. The Legislature believes that such action may prove necessary to the protection of the interests of the Virgin Islands watch industry and its employees.

* * * * *

SECTION 3. That, in the interim, the Governor study the situation and prepare recommendations on this subject to the Legislature in light of such developments as may occur."

In compliance with the above resolution the Governor of the Virgin Islands appointed a special committee to make recommendations with regard to preserving the Virgin Islands watch industry. On August 9, 1965, the special committee submitted its report to the Governor of the Virgin Islands. The committee found "that the present rate of expansion in watch manufacturing holds great dangers to the stability of employment in the Islands and the Islands' commercial relations". It recommended that a $2.50 production tax be placed on all watches manufactured in the Islands. It also recommended that quotas be set for watches shipped to the United States. John J. Kirwin, a member of the special committee, testified on deposition that one of the things that was kept in mind at public hearings and meetings of the committee was to control the volume of watch production in the Virgin Islands to forestall adverse legislation from the Federal Congress. [Deposition of John J. Kirwin, December 22, 1965].

Following the recommendations of the special committee, the Legislature of the Virgin Islands enacted Bill No. 2638 which was approved by the Governor of the Virgin Islands on August 30, 1965. (Supra)

Preliminarily, the Court will not decide the motion of the plaintiff for summary judgment on the constitutional issues raised, the issue with regard to improper influence upon the Governor or the issue of Arbitrary action on the part of the Governor. The sole issue upon which this motion will be decided is whether the Watch Production

Quota Act (Act No. 1518) was in violation of the Organic Act of the Virgin Islands of the United States [June 22, 1936, ch 669, § 36, 49 Stat. 1816, 48 U.S.C.A. 1406i] which provides "[t]hat no new export duties shall be levied in the Virgin Islands except by Congress".

Section 36 of the Organic Act of the Virgin Islands of the United States has not been repealed even though there has been a subsequent act called the "Revised Organic Act of the Virgin Islands". [July 22, 1954, ch 558, § 1, 68 Stat. 497] Therefore, it is still the law that the Legislature of the Virgin Islands has no power to levy new export duties.

The determination which will have to be made is whether the watch production tax is an export duty. An export tax has been defined by the Supreme Court of the United States in *Coe* v. *Errol*, 116 U.S. 517, 526, 29 L.ed. 715, 6 S.C. 475, and in *Turpin* v. *Burgess*, 117 U.S. 504, 506, 29 L.ed. 988, 6 S.C. 835, as a tax levied upon the right to export, or upon goods because of the fact that they are being exported or intended to be exported.

From the history of the Act and from the express provision of the Act, *supra*, it can be seen that the primary purpose of the Act was to limit the exportation of watches from the Virgin Islands to the "Customs area of the United States", to forestall the necessity of the Congress taking away the tariff concessions which the Virgin Islands watch manufacturers enjoyed. There can be no other interpretation of the Watch Production Quota Act than it being an export duty upon watches entering the "customs area of the United States". Such an export duty can only be levied by Congress. From this it follows that the Act is in contravention of § 36 of the Organic Act of the Virgin Islands of the United States, [June 22, 1936, ch 699, 49 Stat. 1816, 48 U.S.C.A. 1406i] and is thus illegal.

For the reasons cited above the motion of the plaintiff for summary judgment is hereby granted because there are no material issues of fact which must be determined by the fact finder. *Rule 56, Federal Rules of Civil Procedure.*

With reference to the motion for summary judgment as to count two of the complaint in which the plaintiff alleges that the Virgin Islands Industrial Incentive Act has been administered in a discriminatory manner, the plaintiff made the following contentions:

1. Similarly situated watch manufacturers presently enjoy tax benefits, thus the failure of the defendants to act on plaintiff's petition discriminates against plaintiff.

2. The plaintiff has complied with all the provisions of the Industrial Incentive Act and thus as a matter of law the Court should order that the plaintiff be granted tax benefits under the Industrial Incentive Act.

The defendants in opposition to the motion for summary judgment as to count two of the complaint contended:

1. The application of the plaintiff was deemed disapproved in November, 1963 and because the appeal period has expired, the Court lacks jurisdiction to entertain this action with respect to the Industrial Incentive Act.

2. The plaintiff is not entitled to the benefits of the Industrial Incentive Act as a matter of right because no contractual obligation exists.

The material facts with regard to count two of the complaint are as follows:

On June 12, 1963 before plaintiff commenced operations in St. Croix, plaintiff filed a formal application with the Virgin Islands Industrial Incentive Board reciting all pertinent information requested by the statute. On September 16, 1963 plaintiff filed a supplemental application attesting to the fact that operations had commenced and listing other pertinent information. On September 17, 1963 public hearings were held with respect to plaintiff's application.

On December 9, 1964, the Industrial Incentive Board through its executive officer notified plaintiff that:

"As you may be aware, a controversy exists over our watch industry in regards to its effect on the mainland. Because of this, all applications were ordered 'frozen' by the Governor and he directed that no further action be taken until the matter is clarified. At the time of this directive by Governor Paiewonsky, a few watchmaking firms had already been granted tax exemption and these grants could not be impaired, but the directive did act as a halt on all applicants still under consideration. This accounts for the apparent disparity among the watch firms. As you can see, however, there was no prejudice or arbitrary action involved. It was simply a matter of not impairing any benefits already granted, but nevertheless withholding the granting of any subsequent benefits until a clean bill of health could be given the industry as a whole.

Recently the Governor has written the Board and proposed an interim relief handling of the firms whose applications are being held in abeyance until the cloud is lifted. Due solely to an overloaded agenda this latter proposal has not been considered as yet by the Board.

This office has again scheduled the watch companies' problem for consideration at the next Executive Session and it is our hope that this time it will be discussed and resolved relative to the issue whether the suggested interim relief can or can not be granted.

In any event, this is the status as to date and should anything at all relative to the subject arise, we shall inform you immediately as to its outcome."

Since December 9, 1964 despite requests of plaintiff for interim relief no action was taken by the Industrial Incentive Board with respect to plaintiff's application for tax exemption and subsidy.

On November 18, 1965 the plaintiff brought this action invoking the jurisdiction of this Court pursuant to Title 33 Virgin Islands Code § 4113 which provides:

"Any person, firm or corporation aggrieved by any action of the Governor under the provisions of this subtitle shall be entitled to judicial review thereof by filing an appeal with the District Court of the Virgin Islands, within 30 days after final decision by the Governor. Upon such review all findings, decisions or determinations by the Governor as to questions of fact shall be deemed final in the absence of conclusive showing to the Court of fraud or misrepresentation."

The Court recognizes that there has been no final decision by the Governor. However, the plaintiff has been aggrieved by the inaction of the Industrial Incentive Board caused by the Governor's freeze on watch manufacturers' applications. The Court is, however, of the opinion that the facts alleged by the plaintiff in its complaint and motion are sufficient to invoke this Court's jurisdiction under Title 5 Virgin Islands Code § 1261 et seq. which is the Uniform Declaratory Judgment Act.

The Court does not agree with defendants' contention that plaintiff's application was denied on November 17, 1963 by operation of law. It is inconceivable to the Court that the Government can lull an applicant into believing that its application is being entertained in the regular course of business and then when the "moment of truth" arrives, advise applicant that its application had been deemed to have been disapproved without notice to the applicant. 33 Virgin Islands Code § 4101(b). In the case at bar the plaintiff was advised that its application was being considered by the Virgin Islands Industrial Incentive Board. Later it was advised by an official of the Industrial Incentive Board that the Governor had ordered a "freeze" on all pending watch manufacturers' tax exemption and subsidy applications. In the opinion of the Court the action of the Governor by his directive is an extension as contemplated by Title 33 Virgin Islands Code § 4101(b).

The Court would like to comment briefly on defendants' contention that plaintiff has not complied with the statutory requirements for tax exemption and is thus not entitled to the Industrial Incentive benefits as a matter of right. Defendants argue that they have no contractual obligation to issue a tax exemption to plaintiff. It is difficult for the Court to adhere to such a contention when Title 33 Virgin Islands Code § 4001 makes it clear as its policy that an industrial or business activity which has met the statutory requirements and which may be determined to promote the public interest by economic development of the Virgin Islands and the establishment or expansion of which requires the stimulus of governmental assistance will be entitled to the benefits of the Act. It is also difficult to adhere to the defendants' argument that the plaintiff's activities do not promote the economic development of the Virgin Islands when it is the same activities with respect to the watch industry which defendants tried to protect by enacting the Watch Production Quota Act. The record is replete with Resolutions of the Virgin Islands Legislature, Acts of the Virgin Islands Legislature, and reports of committees which state that the watch industry is of great benefit to the economy of the Virgin Islands and need to be protected in order to further contribute to the economy of the Virgin Islands. If an industry is of economic benefit to the Virgin Islands, then the individuals or companies which make up that industry must of necessity benefit the Virgin Islands' economy.

It would seem to the Court that if four other watch manufacturers who have received tax exemption and subsidy certificates have been deemed to promote the economic welfare of the Virgin Islands, the plaintiff, as long as it has fulfilled all the statutory requirements, should also be deemed to promote the economic welfare of the Virgin Islands and should thus be granted a tax exemption and subsidy certificate.

The Court realizes that tax exemption is not merely a question of law, but involves many economic factors which are more appropriately the function of those to whom this decision is entrusted, which in the case at bar is the Virgin Islands Industrial Incentive Board and the Governor of the Virgin Islands. However, the Court will not sit idly by and permit those officials who are entrusted to carry out their duties fail to assume those responsibilities given to them by the Legislature of the Virgin Islands.

The Court is of the opinion that the defendants should not be permitted to refuse to entertain plaintiff's application "because the Governor believes that other considerations should enter into its [Industrial Incentive Board's] deliberations and recommendations". *Vitex Manufacturing Co. v. Government of the Virgin Islands*, 351 F.2d 313, —— V.I. —— (1965).

The Court, therefore, shall remand the case to the Industrial Incentive Board to make such recommendations as it may deem proper. The Industrial Incentive Board shall make such recommendations to the Governor of the Virgin Islands within 30 days from the date of this memorandum opinion. The Governor of the Virgin Islands shall act within a reasonable time upon the recommendations of the Industrial Incentive Board. If no action is taken by the Industrial Incentive Board or the Governor within the time prescribed above, the plaintiff shall have the right to reopen these proceedings and seek an order compelling the defendants to grant the tax exemption and subsidy benefits to plaintiff.

Having made the above determinations, the Court is of the opinion that it is not necessary to issue a preliminary injunction. Therefore, plaintiff's motion for a preliminary injunction is denied.

March 14, 1966

/s/ WALTER A. GORDON
Judge of the District Court

APPENDIX D

Memorandum Opinion—June 2, 1966—Virgo

MEMORANDUM OPINION

The plaintiff has brought a motion pursuant to Rule 56 of the Federal Rules of Civil Procedure for a Summary Judgment in its favor for the relief requested in its Complaint. Plaintiff in its Complaint seeks a declaratory judgment that §§ 511 to 518, Chapter 9 Title 33 of the Virgin Islands Code as amended by Act No. 1631 be declared null and void. Plaintiff in its Complaint further seeks a permanent injunction prohibiting the defendant, Virgin Islands Government's employees from enforcing any statute directly or indirectly levying a tax on watches shipped from the Virgin Islands to the United States.

I

The history, in brief, leading to this action is that the plaintiff and defendants herein were similarly plaintiff and defendants in this Court's Case No. 165-1965 testing §§ 511 to 518, Chapter 9, Title 33 of the Virgin Islands Code as created by Bill No. 2638—Sixth Legislature of the Virgin Islands (Exhibit A herein).

On March 14, 1966 this Court issued its Memorandum Decision in said Case No. 165-1965. On March 16, 1966 this Court issued an order granting to plaintiff in that case a Summary Judgment invalidating said law.

On March 16, 1966 in Special Session, the Virgin Islands Legislature passed Act No. 1631 (Exhibit E herein) entitled An Act to Amend Certain Provisions of Chapter 9, Title 33 of the Virgin Islands Code Relating to Production Taxes on Watches Manufactured in the Virgin Islands.

On March 22, 1966 that Act was approved by the Governor of the Virgin Islands.

That Bill amended in particular § 511·(a) and (b); § 513, § 514(a)(b)·(d)(1) and (3) and § 515.

Pursuant to said Act the plaintiff herein was sent a letter dated April 19, 1966 from the Director of the Budget of the Virgin Islands setting forth a list of preliminary regular quotas for April 1, 1966 to March 31, 1967 which list included plaintiff's preliminary regular quota.

On March 29, 1966 plaintiff filed its Complaint in this action. No answer has been filed in this action to date.

On May 9, 1966 plaintiff brought on this motion for Summary Judgment based upon its verified Complaint and attached affidavits. Defendants have filed no opposing affidavits nor documents of any kind.

II

It appears from the record herein that there does not exist material issues of fact in this case and the Court therefore will decide this case pursuant to Rule 56 of the Federal Rules of Civil Procedure.

III

Plaintiff in its Complaint (page 5 paragraph 14) alleges as follows: "The invalidity of Sections 511 to 518, Chapter 9, Title 33 of the Virgin Islands Code, as amended, has been determined by this Court and its Judgment, Exhibit D, is *res adjudicata*." In connection therewith plaintiff in its Complaint also alleges (page 5, paragraph 15): "Sections 511 to 518, Chapter 9, Title 33 of the Virgin Islands Code, as amended, are null and void because they: (a) Contravene the provisions of (i) the Revised Organic Act of the Virgin Islands (48 U.S.C.A. § 1406i) which provides that "no export duties shall be levied in the Virgin Islands except by Congress" . . ."

Defendants raise by oral argument that the Act as amended is a tax upon manufacturing on its face and not a tax upon exports and therefore is valid. Defendants assert that a State can tax manufacturing within its borders and defendants cite Port Construction Co. v. The Government of the Virgin Islands, 237 F. Supp. 486. Defendants' position is that the wording of the amended § 511(a) imposes a tax upon watches, clocks and timing apparatus manufactured in the Virgin Islands when sold or removed for sale, consumption or use and defendants therefore contend that this amendment creates a new tax and that that tax is by the wording of the new Act and upon its face a tax upon manufacturing and that the Court should accept it as such.

IV

The following for comparison are the §§ 511 to 518 of Chapter 9, Title 33 which the Court determined invalid by its order of March 16, 1966 and Act No. 1631 containing the amended sections in issue:

"ACT 1518"

"Sec. 511(a). There shall be imposed upon watches manufactured in the Virgin Islands, when sold or removed for sale, consumption or use, a tax at the rate of $2.50 per watch.

(b). A credit of $2.47 per watch shall be allowed upon:

(1) watches manufactured and sold for disposition in the course of retail trade in the Virgin Islands;

(2) watches manufactured and exported to other than the Customs area of the United States;

(3) watches manufactured pursuant to a quota allocated to such manufacture in accordance with the provisions of sections 512 or 513 of this chapter.

(c). For the purpose of sections 511 through 518 of this chapter, "Watches manufactured in the Virgin Islands" includes not only all watches resulting from the processing of raw materials or other component parts, whether by hand or machinery or both, but also all watches mechanical. or otherwise, or assembly of watch movements with respect to which substantial industrial operations are undertaken in the Virgin Islands which, in the judgment of the Governor of the Virgin Islands, affect the economic stability and the commercial relations of the Virgin Islands.

(d). The manufacturer liable for the payment of tax hereunder shall in each case submit such proof as may be required by the Governor as is satisfactory to establish the rate or rates of tax applicable under subsections (a) and (b) of this section to the watch production of such manufacturer.

(e). It shall be obligatory that the tax imposed by subsection (a) of this section be paid periodically, either by the manufacturer, an immediate or secondary purchaser from the manufacturer, or a contract or common carrier, at such intervals and in accordance with such rules and regulations as shall be adopted pursuant to this title by the Governor.

Sec. 512. An amount of 1,800,000 units of watches is hereby established as the maximum amount of watch production consistent with the protection of the economic stability and commercial relations of the Virgin Islands for the period October 1, 1965, to March 31, 1966. Of this amount, the Governor is authorized to allocate 1,500,000 units among manufacturers of watches having a continuous watch manufacturing and shipping record in the Virgin Islands since October 1, 1964, in accordance with the procedure and criteria set forth in section 514 of this chapter. The remaining

300,000 units of watches is reserved as a quantity to be granted in order to relieve against severe financial hardship, and to permit allocation to new manufacturers. All units of watches allocated as quotas to manufacturers under this section shall be entitled to a $2.47 credit per watch.

Sec. 513(a). For each 12-month period subsequent to March 31, 1966, the Governor shall determine, after due investigation, the total annual consumption of watches of all kinds in the customs area of the United States and shall allocate among the manufacturers of watches in the Virgin Islands on that date in accordance with the criteria set (forth in section 514(b) such number of units as shall total 1/9 of annual consumption.

(b). Of the maximum amount of watch production determined in accordance with subsection (a) of this section, not to exceed five per cent shall be reserved as a quantity to supplement quotas allocated to manufacturers and to relieve against severe financial hardship, in accordance with the provisions of section 515 of this chapter. The Governor is authorized to allocate the remainder among manufacturers of watches in the Virgin Islands in accordance with the procedure and criteria set forth in section 514 of this chapter. All units of watches allocated as quotas to manufacturers under this section shall be entitled to $2.47 credit per watch.

Sec. 514(a). Each person engaged or proposing to engage in the manufacture of watches in the Virgin Islands may apply to the Governor for an allocation of the amount of watch production entitled to the $2.47 credit. Such application shall be in writing, shall be on such forms, and shall contain such information, duly certified by independent accountants or auditors as may be required by the Governor in accordance with the provisions of sections 511 to 518 of this chapter or regulations thereunder.

(b). Except as to such portions thereof as shall have been set aside as a reserve, the total maximum amount of watch production entitled to the $2.47 credit per watch shall be allocated for specific periods among applicants in accordance with the following criteria:

(1) 66⅔ per cent of such amount shall be apportioned among manufacturers in accordance with their respective percentages of total payroll in the Virgin Islands subject to Social Security taxation (exclusive of managerial or administrative personnel) incurred in watch manufacture; for disposition in the course of retail trade in the Virgin Islands; for export to other than the Customs area of the United States; and for watches manufactured pursuant to a quota allocation in accordance with Sections 512 or 513 of this chapter; for such six month period nearest to the beginning of the period involved as the Governor may determine to be feasible.

(2) 33⅔ percent of said amount shall be apportioned among manufacturers in proportion to the total number of watches:

manufactured and sold for disposition in the course of retail trade in the Virgin Islands;

exported to other than the Customs area of the United States; and manufactured and shipped under quota allocation to the Customs area of the United States;

during the same six month period as provided for in (1) above.

(c). The Governor shall have the authority to grant an application on temporary basis during such period as may be necessary to conduct and make determinations in accordance with investigations pursuant to section 513(a) or to make final disposition of application.

(d). The Governor may upon due notice and hearing, refuse an application for an allocation or may revoke, modify or suspend an apportionment made to a manufacturer hereunder as in his judgment may be necessary to protect the economic stability and the commercial relations of the Virgin Islands upon a finding that

(1) the manufacturer is not in good faith organized for the purpose of the manufacture of watches in the Virgin Islands; or

(2) the application is or was made for the purpose of frustrating or defeating the purposes of this Chapter in protecting the economic stability and commercial relations of the Virgin Islands; or

(3) the manufacturer has discontinued the manufacture of watches in the Virgin Islands; except that (i) a temporary interruption of production attributable to normal business reasons shall not be deemed in itself a discontinuance of manufacture of watches within the meaning of this subparagraph, and (ii) nothing in this subparagraph shall prohibit the sale of a business to which a quota has been assigned, but no quota may be purchased or sold apart from the sale of the business;

(4) the manufacturer has misrepresented material facts in connection with his application, or has failed or refused to submit information as required; or

(5) the manufacturer has failed to utilize wholly or partially, the quota assigned to him.

(e). In the apportionment of quotas to a manufacturer hereunder, the Governor is authorized to take into account, and to make a corresponding deduction, watch for watch, where such is in his judgment necessary to protect the economic stability and the commercial relations of the Virgin Islands, of any quantity of watches shipped to the customs area of the United States by the same manufacturer, or a firm corporately or personally affiliated, from any other territory or possession of the United States.

(f). Whenever the Governor shall determine upon due notice and hearing, that all or part of a quota allocated to a manufacturer shall remain unused at the end of a quota period, he may cancel the allocation, in whole or in part, as the case may be, and such allocation, in whole or in part may be reallocated to another manufacturer or placed in the reserves provided for in section 512 or 513(b) of this chapter.

Sec. 515. In making grants out of the reserve amount provided for in sections 512, and 513(b) of this chapter, the Governor shall give special weight to the maintenance and promotion of employment, and to the complete assembly of watches from individual component parts and other characteristics of production contributing special value to the Virgin Islands. The Governor shall also take into account, but is not limited to the consideration of the following factors: investment in plant and equipment for watchmaking in the Virgin Islands; minimum quantities required for production without loss, and abnormal or unforeseeable economic circumstances.

Sec. 516. The Governor is authorized to designate such individuals or groups from time to time as he may deem necessary for the purpose of assisting or advising him in the performance of his duties and responsibilities, and the exercise of his authority under the provisions of sections 511 to 518 of this chapter.

Sec. 517. The Governor shall have authority to issue such rules, regulations and requirements as he may deem necessary or appropriate to effectuate and implement the provisions of sections 511 to 517 of this chapter, including but not limited to the prescribing of forms and requirements of reports and the issuance of stamps or other evidence of payment of taxes.

Sec. 518. Any decision or determination made by the Governor under the provisions of this chapter as to questions of fact shall be deemed final in any proceedings in any court except upon a conclusive showing that such decision or determination was arbitrary or fraudulent. The commencement of any proceedings in any court shall not operate as a stay of collection of any tax imposed by this chapter, or of compliance with any provisions of the same or any rules, regulations or orders issued thereunder.

SECTION 2. This Act shall become effective upon approval by the Governor.

Thus passed by the Legislature of the Virgin Islands on August 25, 1965.

Witness our Hands and the Seal of the Legislature of the Virgin Islands this 25th Day of August, A.D., 1965.''

/s/ EARLE B. OTTLEY
President

/s/ DAVID PURITZ
Legislative Secretary

"Act 1631"*

"Bill No. 2780"

To Amend Certain Provisions of Chapter 9, Title 33 of the Virgin Islands Code Relating to Production Taxes on Watches Manufactured in the Virgin Islands.

BE IT ENACTED by the Legislature of the Virgin Islands:

Section 1. Subsection (a), section 511 of Title 33 of the Virgin Islands Code is hereby amended to read as follows:

"§ 511. (a) There shall be imposed upon watches, clocks and timing apparatus manufactured in the Virgin Islands, when sold, or removed for sale, consumption or use, a tax at the rate of $2.50 per watch."

Section 2. Subsection (b), section 511 of said Title 33 is amended to read:

"(b). For the purpose of sections 511 through 518 of this chapter, 'Watches, clocks and timing apparatus manufactured in the Virgin Islands' includes not only all watches, clocks and timing apparatus resulting from the processing of raw materials or other component parts, whether by hand or machinery or both, but also all watches, clocks and timing apparatus, mechanical or otherwise, or assembly of watch or clock movements or timing apparatus with respect to which substantial industrial operations are undertaken in the Virgin Islands which, in the judgment of the Governor of the Virgin Islands, affect the economic stability and the commercial relations of the Virgin Islands."

---

* Material italicized not in text of Act No. 1631. Omissions indicated by "o" on margin.

Section 3. Subsection 513 of said Title 33 is amended to read as follows:

(a) For each 12-month period subsequent to March 31, 1966, the Governor shall determine, after due investigation, the total annual consumption of watches of all kinds within the customs area of the United States *during the latest calendar year* and shall allocate among manufacturers of watches in the Virgin Islands during each 12-month period subsequent to March 31, 1966, in accordance with the criteria set forth in section 514(b) of this Title, such number of units as shall total 1/9 of such annual consumption. *In the event that total annual consumption of watches of all kinds within the customs area of the United States during the latest calendar year cannot be determined as of April 1 of the year following,* the Governor is authorized to make preliminary and partial allocations *on that date,* which allocations *shall be taken into account when consumption data for such latest calendar year become available. If the annual consumption total for the latest calendar year is revised by the United States Tariff Commission during any such 12-month period, the Governor is authorized to make appropriate and corresponding adjustment of the allocations made to Virgin Islands manufacturers.*

(b) If in any 12-month period subsequent to March 31, 1966, clocks, or timing apparatus other than watches are produced in the Virgin Islands, the Governor shall determine, after due investigation, the total annual consumption of clocks and the total annual consumption of the same or similar timing apparatus in the customs area of the United States and shall allocate among 1) Virgin Islands manufacturers of clocks and/or 2) Virgin Islands manufacturers of timing apparatus other than watches, such number of units as shall total 1/9 of such annual consumption of clocks and such number of units as shall total 1/9 of such timing apparatus other than watches. Such allocations shall be in accordance wtih provisions established herein with respect to watches. In the event that a manufacturer produces more than one category of products for which allocation is to be made, his allocation for each category of product shall be separately determined and an apportionment of his payroll reported under section 514(b)(1) of this Title shall be required to be made, in accordance with such rules and regulations as shall be adopted by the Governor.

(c) Of the maximum amount of production of watches, clocks or timing apparatus determined in accordance with subsections (a) and (b) of this section not to exceed five per cent in each category shall be reserved as a quantity to supplement quotas allocated to manufacturers and to relieve against severe financial hardship, in accordance with the provisions of section 515 of this chapter. The Governor is authorized to allocate the remainder among manufacturers in the Virgin Islands of watches, clocks or timing apparatus in accordance wtih the criteria set forth in section 514 of this chapter. In the event that a manufacturer produces more than one category of products for which an allocation is to be made, his allocation for each category of product shall be separately determined and an apportionment of his payroll reported under section 514(b)(1) of this chapter shall be required to be made in accordance with such rules and regulations as shall be adopted by the Governor.

Section 4. Subsections (a) and (b) of section 514 of said Title 33 are amended to read as follows:

514(a) Each person engaged or proposing to engage in the manufacture of watches, clocks or *tuning* apparatus in the Virgin Islands may apply to the Governor for an allocation of the amount of production *for each such category entitled to the $2.47 credit.* Such application shall be in writing, shall be on such forms, and shall contain such information, duly certified by independent accountants or auditors as may be required by the Governor in accordance with the provisions of sections 511 to 518 of this chapter or regulations thereunder.

(b) *Except as to such portions thereof as shall have been set aside as a reserve, the total maximum amount of watch, clock or timing apparatus production entitled to the $2.47 credit per watch shall be allocated* for specific periods among applicants in accordance with the following criteria:

(1) 66⅔ per cent of such amount shall be apportioned among manufacturers in accordance with their respective percentages of total payroll in the Virgin Islands *subject to Social Security taxation* (exclusive of managerial or administrative personnel) incurred *in manufacture of watches, clocks, or timing apparatus; for disposition in the course of retail trade in the Virgin Islands; for export to other than the Customs area of the United States; and for watches, clocks or timing apparatus manufactured pursuant to a a quota allocation in accordance with sections 512 or 513 of this chapter; for such six-month period nearest to the beginning of the period involved as the Governor may determine to be feasible.*

(2) 33⅔ per cent of said amount shall be apportioned among manufacturers in proportion to

the total number of watches, *clocks or units of timing apparatus;* manufactured and sold for disposition *in the course of retail trade in the Virgin Islands; exported to other than the Customs area of the United States; and manufactured and shipped under quota allocation to the Customs area of the United States; during the same six-month period as provided for in (1) above.*

Section 5. Subparagraphs (1) and (3) of subsection (d), section 514 of said Title 33 are amended to read as follows:

(1) the manufacturer is not in good faith organized for the purpose of the manufacture of watches, clocks or timing apparatus in the Virgin Islands; or

(3) the manufacturer has discontinued the manufacture of watches, clocks or timing apparatus in the Virgin Islands; except that (i) a temporary interruption of production attributable to normal business reasons shall not be deemed in itself a discontinuance of manufacture within the meaning of this subparagraph, and (ii) nothing in this section shall prohibit the sale of a business to which a quota has been assigned, but no quota may be purchased or sold apart from the sale of the business.

Section 6. Subsection (e), section 514 of said Title 33 is amended to read as follows:

(e) In the apportionment of quotas to a manufacturer hereunder, the Governor is authorized to take into account, and to make a corresponding deduction, unit for unit of the category of product, where such is in his judgment necessary to protect the economy stability and the commercial relations of the Virgin Islands, of any quality of watches, clocks or units of timing apparatus *shipped to the customs area of the United States from any other territory or possession of the United States* by the same manufacturer, or by subsidiary wholly or partially owned by it, a corporation with substantially the same stockholders or officers, or any non-corporate business organization a substantial financial interest in which is held by such manufacturer, or by its officers or stockholders.

Section 7. Section 515 of said Title 33 is amended *by deleting from the last sentence thereof the words "for watchmaking".*

Section 8. This Act shall become effective upon approval by the Governor.

February 16, 1966"

V

In comparing the two it will be noted that in both Acts, § 511(a) imposes a tax of $2.50 each upon watches manufactured in the Virgin Islands when sold or removed for sale, consumption or use (clocks and timing apparatus also have been included throughout by Act No. 1631).

The credit in § 511(b) of the previous Act of $2.47 per watch if sold retail in the Virgin Islands, shipped to other than the United States Customs area or manufactured per the quota established was eliminated in the Act in issue and was replaced by § 511(d) which provided that the rate of tax imposed shall be 3¢ per watch, clock or timing apparatus *upon the amount of production* (italics supplied) for each said unit produced within the quota established by the Governor and $2.50 per each said unit in excess.

Section 513(a) as newly amended provides as *did its predecessor* that the *total quota* to be allocated shall equal 1/9 of the total watches *consumed within the Customs Area of the United States* (§ 513(a) of the new Act provides similarly for clocks and timing apparatus).

VI

It is clearly held by the United States Supreme Court in the following cases that the Court in determining the validity of a tax statute shall concern itself with the practical operation of the tax, that is, substance rather than form. American Oil Company v. Neill, 380 U.S. 451, 455 (1965). "In resolving the issue (this Court is) not concluded by the name or description of the tax as found in the act; (this Court's) duty is to ascertain its nature and effect". Stewart Dry Goods Company v. John B. Lewis, 294 U.S. 550-580.

As stated by the United States Supreme Court in Galveston, Harrisburg and San Antonio Railway Co. et al. v. State of Texas, 210 U.S. 217 "Neither the State Court nor the legislatures, by giving the tax a particular name or by the use of some form of words, can take away our duty to consider its nature and effect". See also Postal Telegraph Cable Co. v. Wirt Adams, Revenue Agent of the State of Mississippi, 155 U.S. 688, 698, 39 Led. 311, 316, 15 S. Ct. 268.

Act No. 1631 states at one point that it taxes production of units (§ 511(d) and at another point that it taxes the sale or removal for sale of said items (§ 511(a)).

The Act as amended does not levy a flat tax upon all production nor does it levy a graduating tax upon all production. It does however (as did its predecessor Act) create a quota effecting the tax rate. This quota is geared to *previous annual consumption of watches in the customs area of the United States.* This quota foundation is identical to the quota foundation of the predecessor Act.

Act No. 1631 imposes (as did Act No. 1518) a tax of 3¢ per unit on items within the quota allocation and $2.50 per unit on those items in excess of the quota or to be sold outside of the United States Customs area. This wide tax rate gap is suggestive of a regulatory rather than a revenue raising measure based upon production.

Whatever differences that do exist in the wording of the two Acts either accomplish the same results or are insignificant.

The legislative history of this amended act shows its passage by the Legislature on March 16, 1966 the very same day that this Court declared the original §§ 511 to 518 of Chapter 9, Title 33 to be invalid. The amended Act was approved by the Governor on March 22, 1966.

In 1965 total watch production in the U. S. Virgin Islands approximated 3,671,906 units of which 3,578,000 units were shipped to the United States—in other words approximately 97.4% of the Virgin Islands watch production was shipped to the United States for sale. Therefore, a tax upon watch production in the Virgin Islands or upon watches sold or removed for sale in reality taxes watches exported to the United States Customs area.

VII

The United States Supreme Court has said: "If by varying the form—that is to say, if by using one name for a tax instead of another, or imposing a tax in terms upon one subject where another is in reality aimed at,—the substance and effect of the imposition may be changed, constitutional limitations on powers of taxation would come to naught. The rule is otherwise". . . . "The fact that a tax ostensibly laid upon a taxable subject is to be measured by the value of a non taxable subject at once suggests the probability that it was the latter rather than the former that the lawmaker sought to reach. If inquiry discloses persuasive grounds for the conclusion that such is the real purpose and effect of the legislation, the tax can not be upheld without subverting the well established rule that 'what can not be done directly because of constitutional restriction cannot be accomplished indirectly by legislation which accomplishes the same result' . . . Fairbanks v. United States, 181 U.S. 283, 294, 300

Led. 862, 869, 21 S. Ct. Rep. 648". Macallen Company v. Commonwealth of Massachusetts, 279 U.S. 620 (1929).

Act No. 1631 although somewhat different in language than Act No. 1518 nevertheless has the same effect. The result accomplished is the same result accomplished by Act 1518. This Court therefore must find §§ 511 to 518, Chapter 9, Title 33 of the Virgin Islands Code as amended by Act No. 1631 as invalid as it found said sections created by Act No. 1518 and therefore declare §§ 511 to 518, Chapter 9, Title 33 of the Virgin Islands Code as amended by Act No. 1631 null and void for the reason it is an export duty upon watches entering the Customs area of the United States and by reason thereof said amended Act is in contravention of § 36 of the Organic Act of the Virgin Islands of the United States (June 22, 1936, ch. 699, 49 Stat. 1816, 48 U.S.C. 1406i).

For United States Supreme Court cases in point on this subject see:

Stewart Dry Goods Company v. John B. Lewis, 294 U.S. 550-580 (1935)

Charles I. Dawson, Attorney General of the State of Kentucky et al. v. Kentucky Distilleries and Warehouse Company, 255 U.S. 638, 65 Led. 638, 41 S. Ct. 272

St. Louis Cotton Compress Co. v. State of Arkansas 260 U.S. 346, 67 Led. 297, 43 S. Ct. 126

Samuel C. Cook v. Commonwealth of Pennsylvania, 97 U.S. 566, 24 Led. 1015

Crew Levick Co. v. Commonwealth of Pennsylvania, 245 U.S. 292, 62 Led. 295, 38 S. Ct. 126

Galveston, Harrisburg and San Antonio Railway Co. et al. v. State of Texas, 210 U.S. 217, 52 Led. 1031, 28 S. Ct. 638

This case having been decided on the above grounds, the additional grounds alleged by the plaintiff need not be determined. For the above reasons cited, the motion of the plaintiff for Summary Judgment upon its Complaint seeking a Declaratory Judgment pursuant to 28 U.S.C. 2201-2 and §§ 1261-73, Chapter 89, Title 5 of the Virgin Islands Code, that §§ 511 to 518, Chapter 9, Title 33 of the Virgin Islands Code as amended by Act No. 1631 are invalid, null and void is hereby granted.

This Court has considered Plaintiff's request for injunctive relief and in view of this Court's decision above declaring the amended Act invalid, the Court deems that said injunctive relief is not necessary and Plaintiff's request for said relief is therefore denied.

WALTER A. GORDON
Walter A. Gordon
Judge of the District Court

June 2, 1966

APPENDIX E

UNITED STATES COURT OF APPEALS
FOR THE THIRD CIRCUIT

No. 16116

VIRGO CORPORATION

v.

RALPH M. PAIEWONSKY, Governor, MORRIS F. deCASTRO,
Director of the Budget and the GOVERNMENT OF THE
VIRGIN ISLANDS,

Appellants

No. 16133

MASTER TIME COMPANY, LTD.

v.

PERCY deJONGH, as Commissioner of the Department of
Finance of the Government of the Virgin Islands,

Appellant

No. 16374

VIRGO CORPORATION

v.

RALPH M. PAIEWONSKY, Governor, MORRIS F. DECASTRO,
Secretary, Governor's Committee on the Virgin Islands
Watch Industry, Member, Virgin Islands Industrial In-
centive Board, and Director of the Budget; ALBERT
PRENDERGAST, Member, Governor's Committee on the
Virgin Islands Watch Industry, Chairman, Virgin Is-
lands Industrial Incentive Board, and Commissioner
of Commerce; PERCY DEJONGH, Commissioner of the
Department of Finance; RUBEN WHEATLEY, Member,

Virgin Islands Industrial Incentive Board and Director of Tax Division of Department of Finance; MAHLEN LINDQUIST, Member, Virgin Islands Industrial Incentive Board; ADOLPH POTTER, Member, Virgin Islands Industrial Incentive Board; JOSEPH ALEXANDER, Member, Virgin Islands Industrial Incentive Board; PERCY GARDINE, Member, Virgin Islands Industrial Incentive Board; the GOVERNMENT OF THE VIRGIN ISLANDS, and ATLANTIC TIME PRODUCTS CORPORATION,

Appellants

Appeals From the District Court of the Virgin Islands, Division of St. Croix

---

Argued at Christiansted February 3, 1967
Before STALEY, *Chief Judge,* and MARIS and FREEDMAN, *Circuit Judges.*

Opinion of the Court

(Filed September 29, 1967)

By MARIS, *Circuit Judge.*

These are appeals by the defendants from judgments entered against them in the District Court of the Virgin Islands. The appeals at our docket Nos. 16116, 16133 and 16374 involve the validity of the Watch Production Act of 1965, as originally enacted and as amended, 33 V.I.C. §§ 511-518, which, inter alia, imposed taxes on the production of watches in the Virgin Islands and also involve the validity of the Governor's action in allocating quotas to watch manufacturers under the Act. The appeal at our docket No. 16374 raises, also, the question whether the Governor acted arbitrarily in denying the plaintiff Virgo Corporation tax exemption and subsidy benefits under the Virgin Islands industrial incentive program, 33 V.I.C. §§ 4001 et seq.

Virgo Corporation, a Virgin Islands corporation engaged in the business of manufacturing and selling watches, field a complaint in the district court, at Civil Docket No. 165-1965, Division of St. Croix, against the Government of the Virgin Islands, its Governor, and certain of its other officers, and Atlantic Time Products Corporation. The complaint set out two separate claims for relief. The first was for a determination that the Governor had acted arbitrarily in making an allocation to Atlantic Time Products Corporation, a newly established watch manufacturer, from the reserve quota of 300,000 units established under the Watch Production Act while denying Virgo an allocation of 45,000 additional watches from the reserve quota to relieve it from severe financial hardship. Virgo sought a judgment declaring that the Governor's allocation of 240,000 units to Atlantic Time was invalid and that Virgo was entitled to the allocation of the additional 45,000 units which it had requested. In the alternative, Virgo asked that the entire watch production program and the taxes imposed by the Watch Production Act of 1965 be declared invalid. Virgo's second claim for relief was for a judgment declaring it entitled to tax exemption and subsidy benefits under the Virgin Islands industrial incentive program, 33 V.I.C. §§ 4001 et seq. The district court, after hearing, filed its opinion holding the Watch Production Act of 1965 to be invalid on the ground that it imposed a new export duty in violation of section 36 of the Organic Act of 1936, 49 Stat. 1816-1817. In respect to count two of the complaint, the court concluded that the case should be remanded to the Virgin Islands Industrial Incentive Board with directions that recommendations which the Board deemed proper should be made to the Governor within 30 days, that the Governor should act thereon within a reasonable time thereafter; and that if no action was taken within the time prescribed, Virgo could seek an order compelling the defendants to grant tax exemption and subsidy benefits to it. 5 V.I. 342, 251 F. Supp. 279. The court entered an order pursuant to its opinion on March 16, 1966 from which the defendant appealed to this court at our docket No. 15894. That appeal was, however, dismissed by this court as premature since the Industrial Incentive Board had not yet acted and a final decision on all the claims for relief had accordingly not yet been rendered.

By the Watch Production Act of August 30, 1965,[1] the Legislature sought to discourage through taxation the production of watches[2] destined for ultimate shipment to the United States in amounts in excess of one-ninth of the annual consumption of watches in the United States. For the six months period from October 1, 1965 to March 31, 1966, the Governor of the Virgin Islands was authorized by the Act to assign to watch manufacturers in the Virgin Islands production quotas totaling 1,800,000 units. A tax of $2.50 per watch was imposed on all watches produced in the Virgin Islands upon which tax a credit of $2.47 was to be allowed in the case of all watches manufactured within the quota allocated and watches not destined for the United States. The Governor was authorized to allocate 1,500,000 of the total quota of 1,800,000 units to Virgin Islands manufacturers in accordance with a formula set out in the Act. The remaining 300,000 units were to be reserved to relieve severe financial hardship, and to permit allocation to new manufacturers. The Watch Production Act of 1965 was amended by the Act of March 22, 1966.[3] Under the Act, as amended, the tax of $2.50 per watch was imposed upon all watches produced in the Virgin Islands in excess of the quotas to be allocated by the Governor for manufacture by

---

[1] Act of August 30, 1965, No. 1518, V.I. Sess. L. 1965, pp. 470 et seq.; 33 V.I.C. §§ 511-518.

[2] The term "watches" includes watches, clocks and timing apparatus.

[3] Act of March 22, 1966, No. 1631, V.I. Sess. L. 1966, pp. 98 et seq.

Virgin Islands manufacturers, which were to aggregate one-ninth of the total annual consumption of watches within the customs area of the United States. Watches manufactured within these quotas were to be taxed at 3 cents per watch only.

After the passage of the Act of 1966 Virgo brought a second suit in the district court against the Government of the Virgin Islands, its Governor, and the Director of the Budget, at Civil Docket No. 37-1966, Division of St. Croix, for a judgment declaring the amended Act invalid in that it violated section 36 of the Organic Act of 1936 and section 28(d) of the Revised Organic Act of 1954. The district court held that the statute, as amended, continued the export duty in violation of section 36 of the Organic Act of 1936. 5 V.I. 359, 254 F. Supp. 405. Judgment was entered accordingly in favor of Virgo on June 3, 1966 and an appeal by the defendants at our docket No. 16116 followed.

In compliance with the district court's order of March 16, 1966, the Virgin Islands Industrial Incentive Board held a hearing and recommended to the Governor that partial tax exemption be granted to Virgo. This recommendation the Governor disapproved, however, and he denied Virgo's application for benefits under the industrial incentive program. Virgo then moved in the district court for an order to compel the defendants to grant it the benefits it had applied for. The district court held it was the legislative intent that tax exemption and subsidies be made available to Virgo if it complied with the requirements of the statute and that after such compliance no discretionary power remained in the Governor to deny it benefits under the program. 5 V.I. 417, 259 F. Supp. 26. Accordingly, on November 7, 1966 the court entered an order directing the Governor to issue a certificate granting Virgo the same tax exemptions and subsidy benefits which had been granted to four other watch companies. The defendants thereupon took an appeal at our docket No. 16374 from the orders of March 16, 1966 and November 7, 1966.

Master Time Company, Ltd., a Virgin Islands corporation engaged in the manufacture and sale of watches, brought suit against the Commissioner of the Department of Finance of the Government of the Virgin Islands, at Civil Docket No. 142-1965, Division of St. Croix, for a judgment declaring the Watch Production Act invalid as imposing a prohibited export duty upon goods coming into the United States. On the basis of its conclusions in the actions brought by Virgo, the district court entered judgment in this action in favor of Master Time. 5 V.I. 388, 255 F. Supp. 927. The defendant then took the appeal at our docket No. 16133.

The three appeals now before us, insofar as they relate to the Watch Production Act, raise similar questions. They were consolidated for argument and will be considered together in this opinion. The issues which they raise are (1) whether the Watch Production Act, as originally enacted or as amended, is invalid as imposing an export tax on watches shipped to the United States in excess of the production quotas established under the Act or is otherwise invalid, or (2) if the district court erred in holding the Act invalid, whether the allocation made by the Governor from the reserve quota to Atlantic Time Products Corporation resulted from such non-statutory considerations and improper influences as to render the allocation void. The district court held, and the plaintiffs urge, that the Watch Production Act as amended by the Act of 1966 contained no changes from the original Act which were of legal significance in respect of the issues of validity involved in these appeals. We agree and accordingly will not consider separately the Act as originally enacted in 1965 and as amended in 1966.

I. *Validity of the Watch Production Act.*

The district court held that the Watch Production Act, both as originally enacted and as amended, was invalid because it imposed an export duty upon watches exported from the Virgin Islands to the customs area of the United States in violation of section 36 of the Organic Act of the Virgin Islands of June 22, 1936, 48 U.S.C.A. § 1406i, which the court held to be still in force. That section provided as follows:

"SEC. 36. Taxes and assessments on property and incomes, internal-revenue taxes, license fees, and service fees may be imposed and collected, and royalties for franchises, privilieges, anl concessions granted may be collected for the purposes of the Government of the Virgin Islands as may be provided and defined by the municipal councils herein established: *Provided,* That all money hereafter derived from any tax levied or assessed for a special purpose shall be treated as a special fund in the treasury of the Virgin Islands and paid out for such purpose only, except when otherwise authorized by the legislative authority having jurisdiction after the purpose for which such fund was created has been accomplished. Until Congress shall otherwise provide, all laws concerning import duties and customs in the municipality of Saint Thomas and Saint John now in effect shall be in force and effect in and for the Virgin Islands: *Provided,* That the Secretary of the Treasury shall designate the several ports and sub-ports of entry in the Virgin Islands of the United States and shall make such rules and regulations and appoint such officers and employees as he may deem necessary for the administration of the customs laws in the Virgin Islands of the United States; and he shall fix the compensation of all such officers and employees and provide for the payment of such compensations and other expenses of the collection of duties, fees and taxes imposed under the customs laws from the receipts thereof. The export duties in effect on the date of enactment of this Act may be from time to time reduced, repealed, or restored by ordinance of the municipal council having jurisdiction: *Provided further*, That no new export duties shall be levied in the Virgin Islands except by the Congress." 49 Stat. 1816-1817.

It will be observed that except for the authority conferred upon the Secretary of the Treasury to administer the customs laws of the Virgin Islands, section 36 of the Organic Act of 1936 dealt solely with certain specified powers of the legislative authorities, the municipal councils and the legislative assembly, which the Act created, and with certain limitations upon those powers. Thus the last sentence of the section, upon which the district court relied, dealt solely with the power of the municipal councils to reduce, repeal or restore existing export duties and by a proviso to that grant of power imposed the condition that no new export duties should be levied except by the Congress.

On July 22, 1954 the Congress enacted a Revised Organic Act for the Virgin Islands, 68 Stat. 497, 48 U.S.C.A. §§ 1541 et seq. The Revised Organic Act declared the Virgin Islands to be an unincorporated territory, and completely reorganized its government, abolishing the two existing municipalities with their separate municipal councils and joint legislative assembly, and creating a single territorial government with a single legislature. The Act made comprehensive and complete provisions for the legislative, executive and judicial branches of the government, defining their powers and duties and imposing many specific limitations upon them. In the report of the Senate Committee on Interior and Insular Affairs upon the bill, S. 3378, 83d Congress, which became the Revised Organic Act, it is stated:

"The purpose of S. 3378 is to provide a new organic act, or basic charter of civil government, for the people of the Virgin Islands of the United States. The present act dates from 1936 and is based in no small part on the old Danish colonial system in the islands, which was evolved before the days of modern communication. Substantial changes, political and economical, have taken place in the Virgin Islands in the 18 years since the first somewhat makeshift organic legislation was put together, and under modern conditions the 1936 law is proving unnecessarily cumbersome and inefficient as well as expensive for the mainland taxpayers.

. . .

"S. 3378 would eliminate much of this wasteful duplication in governments and governmental services, thus affording the islands more efficient and more truly representative government. At the same time, it would give a greater degree of autonomy, economic as well as political, to the people of the Virgin Islands." S. Rept. 1271, 83d Cong. pp. 1, 2, 2 U.S. Code, Cong. & Admin. News, 1954, pp. 2585, 2586.

There thus appears to be a clear legislative intent that the Revised Organic Act should become a new basic charter of government for the territory to take the place of the "somewhat makeshift" Organic Act of 1936 which had proved "unnecessarily cumbersome and inefficient" and that the new Act should grant "a greater degree of autonomy, economic as well as political, to the people of the Virgin Islands". In many respects the Revised Organic Act parallels the Organic Act of 1936. But in a great many other instances the provisions of the revised Act diverge from the provisions of the former Act with respect to similar subject matter. We find no indication in the Revised Organic Act that the Congress intended any part of the Act of 1936 to remain in force after the Revised Organic Act took effect, except those provisions of the Act of 1936 which had made certain laws of the United States applicable to the Virgin Islands.[4] This saving provision, which appears in section 8(c) of the Revised Organic Act, 48 U.S.C.A. § 1574 (c), is the only reference in that Act to the Act of 1936.

It is, of course, clear that those provisions of the Act of 1936 which were inconsistent with provisions of the Revised Organic Act were repealed by implication by the latter Act. It is equally true, we believe, that those provisions of the old Act which dealt with and limited the powers of organs of the former municipalities, such as the municipal councils, fell with the abolition of the organs of government to which they related. There is no reason to believe that the Congress, which was intent on providing a greater degree of autonomy to the people of the territory through a newly created territorial legislature, intended to shackle that legislature with restrictions which had been placed in 1936 upon the municipal councils as the direct successors of the Old Danish colonial councils but which the Congress had omitted from the revised Act. Quite the contrary was indicated by the Congress when in section 8(c) of the revised Act it provided:

". . . That the legislature shall have power, when within its jurisdiction and not inconsistent with the other provisions of this Act, to amend, alter, modify, or repeal any local law or ordinance, public or private, civil or criminal, continued in force and effect by this Act, except as herein otherwise provided, and to enact new laws not inconsistent with any law of the United States applicable to the Virgin Islands, subject to the power of Congress to annul any such Act of the legislature." 68 Stat. 501.

---

[4] There is an indication in the legislative history, as noted later in this opinion, that the House of Representatives, at least, intended that the provisions of section 36 of the 1936 Act, which authorized the Secretary of the Treasury to administer the Virgin Islands customs laws should be saved from repeal.

We think, moreover, that in conferring upon the people of the Virgin Islands a new and up-to-date charter of government the Congress could not have intended at the same time to impose upon them the well-nigh impossible task of sorting out those provisions of the old Act which were so inconsistent with the new Act as to be repealed by it from those provisions of the old Act which were to remain in force because they were not sufficiently inconsistent with the new law.[5] The very fact that the Act of 1954 is described in its title as "An Act to revise the Organic Act of the Virgin Islands of the United States" and in its first section as the "Revised Organic Act of the Virgin Islands" indicates that it was intended to supersede and take the place of the Organic Act of 1936 and not merely to amend or repeal portions of it.

It is true that the Revised Organic Act did not expressly repeal the Act of 1936. But in the light of the legislative history of the Act we do not regard this as of controlling significance. For it appears that when the bill, S. 3378, which became the Act of 1954, passed the Senate on May 17, 1954 it contained a section reading as follows:

"SEC. 34. Except to the extent necessary to implement the provisions of section 35, the Act of June 22, 1936 (49 Stat. 1807), and any other provisions of law inconsistent with this Act are hereby repealed." 100 Cong. Rec. 6654.

---

[5] The report of the commission appointed under the authority of section 8(d) of the Revised Organic Act would not be helpful in this regard. For the task of that commission was to determine which general statutes of the United States should be applicable to the Virgin Islands as well as to the rest of the country and which should be declared inapplicable to the Virgin Islands. The commission was not concerned with statutes, such as the organic acts, which were applicable to the Virgin Islands alone.

When S. 3378 came before the House of Representatives on June 22, 1954, the bill was passed by the House after it had substituted in section 34 the following language:

"SEC. 34. Except to the extent necessary to implement the provisions of section 31 hereof and except with reference to the authority of the Secretary of the Treasury under section 36 of the Act of June 22, 1936 (49 Stat. 1807), said act and other provisions of law inconsistent with this act are hereby repealed." 100 Cong. Rec. 8673.

It will thus be seen that except for three specific provisions, both Houses clearly expressed in precise language their intention to repeal the Act of 1936. Nonetheless, although except as to the three provisions referred to in the language above quoted the two Houses were in agreement on the repeal of the Act of 1936, the bill reported from the Conference Committee of the two Houses which became the Revised Organic Act did not contain an express repealing section. No explanation of this omission appears in the statement of the House Conferees or anywhere else in the legislative history and it well may be that it was omitted inadvertently in the pressure of legislative business or that it was deemed unnecessary in view of the purpose of the Act and its structure as a complete revision of the organic law.

It thus seems clear that the Revised Organic Act of 1954 operated to repeal the Organic Act of 1936. But even if it be assumed that the Revised Organic Act did not have this effect there is another basis for concluding that the legislative power of the Virgin Islands Legislature is not limited by the provisions of section 36 of the Organic Act of 1936 which restricted the legislative power of the former municipal councils. When originally enacted the Revised Organic Act of 1954 described the legislative authority and power of the Virgin Islands which it vested in the newly created Legislature in section 8(a) as follows:

"SEC. 8(a). The legislative authority and power of the Virgin Islands shall extend to all subjects of local aplication not inconsistent with this Act or the laws of the United States made applicable to the Virgin Islands, . . ." 68 Stat. 500.

This grant of power was identical with that contained in section 19 of the Organic Act of 1936. 49 Stat. 1811. However, following the decision of the Supreme Court in Granville-Smith v. Granville-Smith, 1955, 349 U.S. 1, the Congress by the Act of August 28, 1958, Pub. L. 85-851, sec. 2, amended the foregoing language of section 8(a) to read as follows:

"The legislative authority and power of the Virgin Islands shall extend to all rightful subjects of legislation not inconsistent with this Act or the laws of the United States made applicable to the Virgin Islands, . . ." 72 Stat. 1094.

The purpose of this amendment was stated in the report of the Senate Committee on Interior and Insular Affairs upon the bill, H.R. 12303, which became the Act of August 28, 1958, as follows:

"Section 2 amends section 8(a) of the existing law under which Territorial legislature's power extends 'to all subjects of local application.' The amendment would make this read: 'to all rightful subjects of legislation.' In *Granville-Smith* v. *Granville-Smith*, 349 U.S. 1 (1955), the Supreme Court held that, at least with respect to persons who are not permanent residents of the islands, the phrase 'subjects of local application' has a meaning narrower than the phrase 'rightful subjects of legislation.' The latter language is used in the Organic Acts of Alaska and Hawaii.

"The committee is of the opinion that the term 'rightful subjects of legislation' is well known in the law, and its application to the legislative power of the Territory should prevent the development of a jurisdictional no man's land where neither Federal nor Territorial law can apply. Under the language of section 2 of the bill, the legislative jurisdiction of the Territory would cover the ordinary area of sovereign legislative power as limited and circumscribed by the Revised Organic Act or the laws of the United States made applicable to the Virgin Islands. The Congress retains, of course, the power to disapprove, modify, and supersede any and all acts of the Territorial legislature." S. Rept. 2267, 85th Cong., p. 2; 3 U.S. Code, Cong. & Admin. News, 1958, p. 4335.

It thus appears that the purpose of the amendment was to broaden the legislative power of the Virgin Islands to cover "the ordinary area of sovereign legislative power" limited only by the provisions of the Revised Organic Act and laws of the United States made applicable to the Virgin Islands. By the latter phrase, of course, is meant those federal statutes applicable to the United States generally which, either by their own terms or by other legislation, are also made applicable to the Virgin Islands. There is no intimation in the amendatory Act or in the committee report that the broader legislative power granted by the amendment was to be limited by provisions of the Organic Act of 1936 which had not been carried over into the Revised Organic Act. Indeed the language used in the report indicated the contrary. It follows that the presently existing power of the Virgin Islands Legislature to deal with all rightful subjects of legislation is not limited by the provisions of section 36 of the Organic Act of 1936.

The precise question to which we address ourselves at this point is whether the limiting proviso of the final sentence of section 36 of the Organic Act of 1936 was operative in 1965 and 1966 to render invalid the enactment by the Legislature of the Watch Production Act and its amendatory Act, assuming that the tax which these Acts levied was an export duty. For the reasons which we have stated we conclude that it was not operative as a limitation upon the power of the Legislature in those years and that the district court erred in holding that it operated to invalidate the Watch Production Act of 1965 and the amendatory Act of 1966.

We think, furthermore, that the district court was wrong in regarding the tax imposed by the Watch Production Act and its amendment as an export duty. For the tax was essentially an excise tax levied on the production of watches in the Virgin Islands, a process local in nature and complete in itself. Articles do not acquire the character of exports while still in the manufacturing process and before they enter the stream of commerce. The tax on the production of watches was aimed at a matter of local concern and was imposed on the manufacture of those articles, not upon their transmission out of the Virgin Islands. The Supreme Court has defined the export process to be the act of carrying or sending abroad, as follows:

"To export means to carry or send abroad; to import means to bring into the country. Those acts begin and end at water's edge. The broader definition which appellant tenders distorts the ordinary meaning of the terms. It would lead back to every forest, mine, and factory in the land and create a zone of tax immunity never before imagined. For if the handling of the goods at the port were part of the export process, so would hauling them to or from distant points or perhaps mining them or manufacturing them. The phase of the process would make no difference so long as the goods were in fact committed to export or had arrived as imports." Canton Railroad Co. v. Rogan, 1951, 340 U.S. 511, 515.

What the Supreme Court said in *Empresa Siderurgica v. Merced County*, 1949, 337 U.S. 154, 156-157, is applicable here:

" '. . . goods do not cease to be part of the general mass of property in the State, subject, as such, to its jurisdiction, and to taxation in the usual way, until they have been shipped, or entered with a common carrier for transportation to another State, or have been started upon such transportation in a continuous route or journey.' *Coe* v. *Errol*, 116 U.S. 517, 527. That test was fashioned to determine the validity under the Commerce Clause of a nondiscriminatory state tax. But as we noted in *Richfield Oil Corp.* v. *State Board*, 329 U.S. 69, 79, it is equally applicable to cases arising either under Art. I, § 10, Cl. 2 (the Import-Export Clause) or under Art. I, § 9, Cl. 5, which prohibits Congress from laying any tax on 'Articles exported from any State.'

"Under that test it is not enough that there is an intent to export, or a plan which contemplates exportation, or an integrated series of events which will end with it. . . . The tax immunity runs to the process of exportation and the transactions and documents embraced in it. . . . Delivery of packages to an exporting carrier for shipment abroad . . . and the delivery of oil into the hold of the ship furnished by the foreign purchaser to carry the oil abroad . . . have been held sufficient. It is the entrance of the articles into the export stream that marks the start of the process of exportation. Then there is certainty that the goods are headed for their foreign destination and will not be diverted to domestic use. Nothing less will suffice.

"So in this case it is not enough that on the tax date there was a purpose and plan to export this property. Nor is it sufficient that in due course that plan was fully executed. . . ."

This test is applicable in the cases now under review. The watches produced in the Virgin Islands when subjected to the taxes imposed under the Watch Production Act had not ceased to be part of the general property within the Territory subject to its taxation. The controlling fact is that the taxes attached while the watches were in the process of their manufacture and before their sale and possible export. It follows that the taxes imposed under the Watch Production Act were not export duties.

Both Virgo and Master Time further urge that the Watch Production Act was invalid because it violated section 28(d) of the Revised Organic Act which, as amended by section 402(a) of the Customs Simplification Act of September 1, 1954, provided:

"All articles coming into the United States from the Virgin Islands shall be subject to or exempt from duty as provided for in section 301 of the Tariff Act of 1930 and subject to internal-revenue taxes as provided for in section 7652(b) of the Internal Revenue Code of 1954." 68 Stat. 1140.

Section 301 of the Tariff Act of 1930 as added by the Customs Simplification Act of 1954, sec. 401, 68 Stat. 1139-1140, was concerned only with the duty upon articles imported from insular possessions, including the Virgin Islands, outside the customs territory of the United States and provided that articles grown, manufactured or produced in any such possession which did not contain foreign materials to the value of more than 50% of their total value should be exempt from duty. Section 301 was repealed by the Tariff Classification Act of 1962, 76 Stat. 72, 75, and these provisions now appear in paragraph 3(a) of the general headnotes and rules of interpretation to the

Tariff Schedules of the United States published by the President, 28 F.R. 8625, 77A Stat. 11.

Paragraphs (1) and (2) of section 7652(b) of the Internal Revenue Code of 1954 provide:

"(b) Virgin Islands.—

"(1) Taxes imposed in the United States.—Except as provided in section 5314, there shall be imposed in the United States, upon articles coming into the United States from the Virgin Islands, a tax equal to the internal revenue tax imposed in the United States upon like articles of domestic manufacture.

"(2) Exemption from tax imposed in the Virgin Islands.—Such articles shipped from such islands to the United States shall be exempt from the payment of any tax imposed by the internal revenue laws of such islands."

Paragraph (3) of section 7652(b) provides for the payment over to the Government of the Virgin Islands of substantial amounts, computed as therein provided, of the taxes collected by the Secretary of the Treasury under paragraph (1) on articles coming to the United States from the Virgin Islands.

It is perfectly clear that the provisions of paragraph (a) of general headnote 3 of the Tariff Schedules of the United States, concerning rates of duty on products of insular possessions, have no bearing on the present question. This is equally true, we think, of the provisions of section 7652(b) of the Internal Revenue Code. For the obvious purpose of paragraph (2) of that subsection is to insure that articles coming from the Virgin Islands to the United States which are taxed in the United States under paragraph (1) shall not also be taxed in the Virgin Islands. The purpose, in other words, was to prohibit double taxation of the same article. The use in paragraph (2) of the word "Such" in the phrase "Such articles shipped from such islands to the United States" makes it clear that the reference is only to those articles shipped from the Virgin Islands to the United States which are described as taxable in paragraph (1). It is not suggested that internal revenue taxes are imposed in the United States upon the domestic manufacture of watches, clocks and timing apparatus. We conclude, therefore, that the Watch Production Act is not invalid by reason of section 28(d) of the Revised Organic Act.

There can be no question as to the power of the legislature of the Virgin Islands to impose an excise tax upon the manufacture of watches in the Territory. The power to impose taxes is a part of the legislative power granted by the Revised Organic Act to the territorial legislature and it has always been recognized as a rightful subject of legislation. H. I. Hettinger & Co. v. Municipality of St. Thomas & St. John, 3 Cir. 1951, 2 V.I. 509, 187 F.2d 774; Port Construction Co. v. Government of Virgin Islands, 3 Cir. 1966, 5 V.I. 549, 558-559, 359 F.2d 663, 667-668. The plaintiffs urge, however, that this particular taxing statute was not a rightful subject of legislation because its purpose and effect were solely to curtail the shipment to the United States of watches produced in the Virgin Islands in numbers in excess of one-ninth of the total United States consumption of watches, and thereby to forestall Congressional action which might render impossible the continuance of the Virgin Islands watch industry. It is certainly true that the Legislature had this possibility in mind in enacting the statute. The record is abundantly clear as to this. Section 301 of the Tariff Act of 1930, as added in 1954, permitted articles manufactured in the Virgin Islands with foreign materials to be admitted duty-free into the United States, provided the value of the foreign materials incorporated into the article did not exceed 50% of the total value of the article. Under this Congressional authority an industry was started in 1959 in the Virgin Islands of assembling watches with foreign materials not exceeding 50% of their finished value and exporting them to the United States duty-free. 4,900 watches were produced in the first year but by 1964 the Virgin Islands production had grown to 2,400,000 units, approximately 9% of the annual watch consumption of the United States. This rapid growth in shipments of duty-free watches from the Virgin Islands came to be regarded by the watch manufacturers of the United States as a serious threat to their industry. Proposals were made in Congress of legislation to terminate the duty-free importation of watches from the Virgin Islands. This possibility greatly concerned the Virgin Islands Legislature which authorized the Governor to study the problem and prepare recommendations. It was pursuant to the Governor's recommendation, made after study by a special committee which he appointed, that the Legislature passed the Watch Production Act of 1965.

It is thus clear that one of the purposes of the Legislature in enacting the Watch Production Act was to discourage the production of watches in the Virgin Islands in quantities so large that their subsequent flooding of the United States market might bring about Congressional withdrawal of the duty-free importation privilege and the consequent destruction of the local industry by this elimination of its principal economic support. But this is not to say that the legislation was invalid as dealing with a prohibited subject. For all that the statute did in mandatory terms was to impose a tax upon the local production of watches at two rates, a low rate upon watches produced within the limited quotas fixed under the Act (and in the original Act on two other minor categories) and a high rate on watches produced in excess of these amounts. While, as we have seen, the Legislature undoubtedly hoped that the imposition of the tax would discourage manufacturers from producing for future shipment to the United States more watches than the quota amounts, it did not actually forbid such production or shipment which all manufacturers remained free to engage in if they chose to do so.

A taxing statute is not invalidated by the fact that it has a collateral purpose and is designed to have a regulatory effect which the legislature desires to achieve. In Magnana Co. v. Hamilton, 1934, 292 U.S. 40, 47, the Court said:

> "From the beginning of our government, the courts have sustained taxes although imposed with the collateral intent of effecting ulterior ends which, considered apart, were beyond the constitutional power of the lawmakers to realize by legislation directly addressed to their accomplishment."

And, to the same effect, see United States v. Sanchez, 1950, 340 U.S. 42, 44, in which case the Court said:

> "It is beyond serious question that a tax does not cease to be valid merely because it regulates, discourages, or even definitely deters the activities taxed. . . . The principle applies even though the revenue obtained is obviously negligible, . . . or the revenue purposes of the tax may be secondary, . . ."

These principles are controlling here. The taxes here involved were imposed upon all watches produced within the Virgin Islands by Virgin Islands manufacturers, a legitimate exercise of the taxing power of the Legislature, despite its collateral regulatory purpose and effect. We cannot say that the low tax of 3 cents on watches within the quota as contrasted with the much higher tax of $2.50 imposed on watches produced in excess of the quota was so palpably arbitrary and unreasonable as to amount to a denial of due process of law. Compare, for example, the $600 license fee imposed by the Territory of Hawaii on a person engaged in the occupation of auctioneer in the district of Honolulu with the $15 fee imposed in other taxation districts, which was upheld by the Supreme Court as not being an arbitrary classification or discriminatory as between persons engaged in the same occupation in the Territory of Hawaii. Toyota v. Hawaii, 1912, 226 U.S. 184.

Nor can we agree with the plaintiffs that the tax on the production of watches in the Virgin Islands was a burden on interstate commerce. The tax in question was imposed, as we have seen, on the production of watches within the Virgin Islands, a process essentially local in character and complete in itself. It is settled that commerce follows after manufacture and is not a part of it. United States v. E. C. Knight Co., 1895, 156 U.S. 1, 12. In other words, commerce does not begin until after manufacture is finished, and hence the commerce clause does not prevent a state from exercising exclusive control over the manufacture. Utah Power & Light Co. v. Pfost, 1932; 286 U.S. 165, 181. Accordingly, the tax on the production of watches in the Virgin Islands was not a tax directly burdening interstate commerce, even though most of the watches taxed were destined for subsequent transportation to the mainland.

We conclude that the Watch Production Act of 1965, both as originally enacted and as amended in 1966,[6] was a rightful subject of legislation within the authority delegated by Congress to the Virgin Islands Legislature and did not violate the commerce clause of the Constitution or the due process clause of the Revised Organic Act.

II. Validity of the Governor's Allocation of Quotas.

In its original suit in the district court at No. 165-1965, Division of St. Croix, Virgo attacked the validity of the action of the Governor in awarding to a new manufacturer,

----

[6] We note as a matter of interest, although it has no bearing on these appeals, that the Act was repealed by the Act of January 27, 1967, No. 1835, as of January 1, 1967, the effective date of the Act of Congress of November 10, 1966, P.L. 89-805, 80 Stat. 1521, which placed a limit upon the number of watches containing foreign components to be admitted from the Virgin Islands to the United State free of duty.

defendant Atlantic Time Products Corporation, 240,000 units out of the 300,000 units reserved by the Watch Production Act, as originally enacted, to be granted by the Governor "to relieve against severe financial hardship, and to permit allocation to new manufacturers." 33 V.I.C. § 512. Virgo also attacked the Governor's action in refusing an additional allocation of 45,000 units to it from the reserve units to relieve it from severe financial hardship.

It appears that the Governor considered the applications of Virgo and others for hardship allocations of additional units as well as the applications of Atlantic Time and other new manufacturers for quota allocations and on September 16, 1965 entered an order denying the applications of Virgo and certain other existing manufacturers for allocations of additional units because of alleged severe financial hardship and granted the applications of Atlantic Time and certain other new manufacturers for production quotas. In his order the Governor stated that the requests of Virgo and others for hardship quotas "shall not be considered at this time as they are all beneficiaries of regular quotas which were issued on September 9, 1965 out of the 1,500,000 units fixed by Act No. 1518 for manufacturers who have had a continuous record of production since October 1, 1964." With respect to the quotas requested by Atlantic Time and two other new manufacturers he said: "That the requests for quotas for new manufacturers are hereby approved in the quantities stated below for the following companies now in production based on present investment, employment, and other factors and criteria as provided by Act No. 1518:

Watches Incorporated	5,000 units
Atlantic Time Products Corporation	240,000 units
Virgiline Watch Company, Inc.	24,000 units."

Subsequently on October 20, 1965 the Governor allotted the remaining 31,000 units of the statutory reserve to another new manufacturer Belmont Industries, Inc.

The Watch Production Act provided that in making grants out of the reserve amount the Governor should give special weight to the "maintenance and promotion of employment" and to "the complete assembly of watches from individual component parts and other characteristics of production contributing special value to the Virgin Islands." The Governor was also to take into account, but was not limited to the consideration of, the following factors: investment in plant and equipment for watchmaking in the Virgin Islands, minimum quantities required for production without loss, and abnormal or unforseeable economic circumstances. 33 V.I.C. § 515. It is clear that while indicating certain factors for his consideration the Act vested in the Governor a very wide discretion in the evaluation of these and all other factors in determining, in the interest of the economic stability and commercial relations of the Virgin Islands, the appropriate allocation of the reserve units. The record indicates that the Governor did consider a wide range of factors in finding that the interests of the Virgin Islands required that the entire reserve should be allotted to new manufacturers and that existing manufacturers alleging hardship did not have an equal claim to it. Under the express terms of the Act this finding is final and unreviewable except upon a conclusive showing that it was arbitrary or fraudulent. 33 V.I.C. § 518. We have carefully examined the voluminous record but find nothing which would support Virgo's contention that the Governor's finding in this regard was arbitrary or fraudulent. Virgo's contention that the Governor's allocation of 240,000 units to Atlantic Time Products Corporation was invalid and that he should have allocated 45,000 units to it must accordingly be rejected.

III. Virgo's Claim for Tax Exemption and Subsidy Benefits.

In its suit in the district court at Docket No. 165-1965, Division of St. Croix, Virgo also sought a declaration that it was entitled to tax exemption and subsidy benefits under the Virgin Islands industrial incentive program, 33 V.I.C. §§ 4001 et seq., or, in the alternative, an order directing the Virgin Islands Industrial Incentive Board and the Governor to take appropriate action on its application for tax exemption and subsidy benefits. As we have seen the court ordered the Board to consider the application and make recommendations to the Governor. The Board thereupon recommended a partial tax exemption which the Governor disapproved for the reason, stated in his letter of disapproval of September 16, 1966, "that the corporation, as evidenced by its substantial profit return, does not require the stimulus of governmental assistance as provided for by the law." The district court on November 7, 1966 entered the order directing the Governor to grant tax exemption and subsidy benefits which is one of the orders now before us for review. We are satisfied that the Governor acted within his discretionary power in denying Virgo's application and that the district court erred in holding to the contrary and in ordering him to grant it.

Section 4001(a) of the Industrial Incentive Act, 33 V.I.C. § 4001(a), states it to be the policy of the Government of the Virgin Islands that "tax exemption and subsidy benefits be made available for the promotion of such industrial or business activities as may be determined will promote the public interest by economic development of the Virgin Islands, and the establishment or expansion of which *require the stimulus of such governmental assistance*" [Emphasis supplied.] It was in the exercise of his judgment as to the applicability of the criterion embodied in the final clause above quoted that the Governor denied Virgo's application. The truth of his finding that Virgo did not require the financial stimulus provided by tax exemption and subsidy benefits is not challenged in this record. On the contrary Virgo's contention is that the clause in question had somehow been repealed by inference by the Act of April 1, 1964, V.I. Sess. L., 65, which deleted certain phrases from other sections of the Act. We find this argument wholly unconvincing.

Virgo also contends that when it made application for benefits under the industrial incentive program and made the showing required by the Act, a contractual obligation immediately arose on the part of the Government of the Virgin Islands to grant it those benefits, which obligation the district court properly enforced by its order. In support of this proposition Virgo cites our decision in Vitex Manufacturing Co. v. Government of Virgin Islands, 3 Cir. 1965, 5 V.I. 429, 351 F.2d 313. However in the Vitex case a wholly different situation was presented. There a certificate granting tax exemption and subsidy benefits had been issued to Vitex, which under the statute did become a contractual obligation of the government, and the question involved in the case was whether, the grant having been made, its subsequent revocation had been in accordance with the law.

The question involved in the present case was answered by this court in Pentheny, Ltd. v. Government of Virgin Islands, 3 Cir. 1966, 5 V.I. 575, 360 F.2d 786. In that case we had occasion to consider whether vested rights to tax exemption and subsidies were acquired by the mere application therefor. While the rights claimed in the Pentheny case arose under the Act of July 5, 1957, No. 224, V.I. Sess. L., p. 146, a predecessor of the statute here under consideration, the provisions upon which the applicant in that case relied were in terms substantially similar to the provisions in the present Act. In that case, it will be recalled, the applicant had invested substantial amounts of capital to construct an office building. During the pendency of the application a new statute, Act No. 798, V.I. Sess. L. 1961, p. 251, became effective which omitted persons engaged in the business of constructing or operating commercial buildings from the category of those who could apply for benefits under the industrial incentive program. This court held that final disposition of a pending application did not take place until the Governor acted upon it, until which time the applicant did not have an order which could be judicially reviewed, and that although the Act of 1957 held forth a possibility of tax exemption and industrial subsidy benefits, the plaintiff had not acquired any vested right thereto merely by applying for them. We referred to the distinction made by the Supreme Court in Wisconsin & M.R. Co. v. Powers, 1903, 191 U.S. 379, between an exemption from taxation contained in a special charter, which would be equivalent to the order or certificate granting tax exemption and subsidies under the industrial incentive program, and an exemption offered as general encouragement to all persons to engage in a certain class of enterprise. And, we continued, "The court stated that the latter was addressed to no one in particular and constituted a mere announcement of policy, not a contract, . . . 'a circumstance to take into account in determining whether the state has purported to bind itself irrevocably or merely has used words of prophecy, encouragement, or bounty, holding out a hope but not amounting to a covenant.' " 5 V.I. 575, 581-582, 585; 360 F.2d 786, 789-790, 791-792.

Under the industrial incentive program there are two separate considerations involved in granting tax exemption and subsidy benefits to newly established enterprises in the Virgin Islands. First, it must appear that the applicant has fully met the objective criteria required of applicants by the Act. But also it must appear that the applicant's business or industry will promote the public interest by economic development of the Virgin Islands and that its establishment or expension will require the stimulus of the assistant authorized by the Act. Since the basic purpose of the industrial incentive program was to advance the economic development of the Virgin Islands, grants of public funds or property to private persons to assist in the establishment or support of an enterprise must be to the advantage of the public. Such grants are necessarily closely articulated with the purposes of the program and are not intended as mere gratuities or bounties. King

Christian Enterprises v. Government of Virgin Islands, 3
Cir. 1965, 5 V.I. 170, 345 F.2d 633; Dorem Corporation v.
Government of the Virgin Islands, 3 Cir. 1966, 5 V.I. 503,
358 F.2d 693, In re Hooper's Estate, 3 Cir. 1966, 5 V.I. 518,
528-530, 359 F.2d 569, 575-576. It is, therefore, only if and
when the Governor, upon considering the Board's recommendations, finds that both sets of criteria have been met
and issues a certificate granting benefits under the program that a contractual obligation arises. It follows that
the district court erred in holding that Virgo had an en-
forceable contract. Virgo further argues that the Governor
improperly denied plaintiff's application as a result of
political considerations. The short answer to this contention is that the Governor stated in writing the reasons
for his action, which adequately supported it, and political
considerations were not among them. We cannot look into
the Governor's mental processes nor speculate as to what
they were.

Finally, it is contended that the non-issuance of a certificate of tax exemption and subsidy benefits when such
benefits had previously been granted to four similarly situated competitors of the plaintiff was a denial of equal protection of the laws in violation of the bill of rights contained
in section 3 of the Revised Organic Act, 48 U.S.C.A. § 1561.
We had occasion in Port Construction Co. v. Government
of Virgin Islands, 1966, 5 V.I. 549, 558-559, 359 F.2d 663,
667-668, to observe that the equal protection clause does
not impose a rigid rule of equality of taxation. It does not
prohibit those inequalities which may result from singling
out one particular class for taxation or exemption therefrom. Only if it appears that there is no rational basis
for the classification so that it is patently arbitrary may
it be set aside as unconstitutionally discriminatory. Even
singling out a group of taxpayers for special relief con-
ditioned upon a showing of individual hardship is not
necessarily invalid. Jefferson Constr. Overseas, Inc. v.

Government of V.I., 3 Cir. 1966, 5 V.I. 543, 359 F.2d 668. Accordingly, the Government of the Virgin Islands is not bound to grant benefits under the industrial incentive program to all who apply for such benefits merely because it had earlier encouraged the establishment of other similar industries by granting such benefits to them. The expressed legislative intent in establishing the program was "to promote the economic development of the Virgin Islands by the offering of certain incentives to the establishment or expansion of industries or businesses." 33 V.I.C. § 4001(a). But it does not follow that once such a benefit has been granted to a certain type of business or industry a procession of similar industries may follow in its train. On the contrary, the Board and the Governor is entitled to consider each applicant on his individual merits in the light of the extent to which his business or industry will promote the public interest by economic development of the Virgin Islands. 33 V.I.C. §§ 4041, 4104. We conclude that the district court erred in setting aside the decision of the Governor denying the plaintiff the tax exemption and subsidy benefits and ordering him to grant them.

The judgments and orders appealed from will be reversed and the causes remanded with directions to dismiss the complaints.

A True Copy:

Teste:

Clerk of the United States Court of Appeals for the Third Circuit.

APPENDIX F

UNITED STATES COURT OF APPEALS FOR THE THIRD CIRCUIT

No. 16,133

MASTER TIME COMPANY, LTD.

vs.

THE HONORABLE PERCY DEJONGH, as Commissioner, Department of Finance of the Government of the Virgin Islands, *Appellant*

(D. C. Civil Action No. 142-1965)

On Appeal From the District Court of the Virgin Islands Division of St. Croix, Christiansted Jurisdiction

Present: Staley, *Chief Judge,* and Maris and Freedman, *Circuit Judges.*

Judgment

This cause came on to be heard on the record from the District Court of the Virgin Islands, Division of St. Croix, Christiansted Jurisdiction and was argued by counsel.

On consideration whereof, it is now here ordered and adjudged by this Court that the judgment and order of the said District Court, filed June 24, 1966, be, and the same are hereby reversed, with costs, and the cause remanded with directions to dismiss the complaint.

Attest:

THOMAS F. QUINN
Clerk

September 29, 1967

APPENDIX G

UNITED STATES COURT OF APPEALS FOR THE THIRD CIRCUIT

No. 16,133

MASTER TIME COMPANY, LTD.

v.

THE HONORABLE PERCY DEJONGH, as Commissioner, Department of Finance of the Government of the Virgin Islands, *Appellant*

Sur Petition for Rehearing

Present: STALEY, *Chief Judge,* and MARIS, McLAUGHLIN, KALODNER, HASTIE, SMITH, FREEDMAN, SEITZ and VAN DUSEN, *Circuit Judges.*

The petition for rehearing filed by Master Time Company, Ltd. in the above entitled case having been submitted to the judges who participated in the decision of this court and to all the other available circuit judges of the circuit in regular active service, and no judge who concurred in the decision having asked for rehearing, and a majority of the circuit judges of the circuit court in regular active service not having voted for rehearing by the court in banc, the petition for rehearing is denied.

By the Court,

MARIS
Circuit Judge

Dated: November 7, 1967

APPENDIX H

Virgin Islands Code

§ 36. [Taxes and fees; power to assess and collect; ports of entry; export duties]

Taxes and assessments on property and incomes, internal-revenue taxes, license fees, and service fees may be imposed and collected, and royalties for franchises, privileges, and concessions granted may be collected for the purposes of the Government of the Virgin Islands as may be provided and defined by the municipal councils herein established: *Provided,* That all money hereafter derived from any tax levied or assessed for a special purpose shall be treated as a special fund in the treasury of the Virgin Islands and paid out for such purpose only, except when otherwise authorized by the legislative authority having jurisdiction after the purpose for which such fund was created has been accomplished. Until Congress shall otherwise provide, all laws concerning import duties and customs in the municipality of Saint Thomas and Saint John now in effect shall be in force and effect in and for the Virgin Islands: *Provided,* That the Secretary of the Treasury shall designate the several ports and sub-ports of entry in the Virgin Islands of the United States and shall make such rules and regulations and appoint such officers and employees as he may deem necessary for the administration of the customs laws in the Virgin Islands of the United States; and he shall fix the compensation of all such officers and employees and provide for the payment of such compensations and other expenses of the collection of duties, fees, and taxes imposed under the customs laws from the receipts thereof. The export duties in effect on the date of enactment of this Act may be from time to time reduced, repealed, or restored by ordinance of the municipal council having jurisdiction: *Provided further,* That no new export duties shall be levied in the Virgin Islands except by the Congress.—June 22, 1936, ch. 699, § 36, 49 Stat. 1816.

67a

APPENDIX I

Virgin Islands Organic Act—Amendments

For Legislative History of Act, see p. 4334

PUBLIC LAW 85-851; 72 STAT. 1094

[H. R. 12303]

An Act to amend the Revised Organic Act of the Virgin Islands.

Be it enacted by the Senate and House of Representatives of the United States of America in Congress assembled, That:

Section 3 of the Revised Organic Act of the Virgin Islands [54] is amended by adding at the end thereof the following new paragraph:

"No political or religious test other than an oath to support the Constitution and the laws of the United States applicable to the Virgin Islands, and the laws of the Virgin Islands, shall be required as a qualification to any office or public trust under the Government of the Virgin Islands."

Sec. 2. Subsection (a) of section 8 of said Act [55] is amended to read as follows:

"(a) The legislative authority and power of the Virgin Islands shall extend to all rightful subjects of legislation not inconsistent with this Act or the laws of the United States made applicable to the Virgin Islands, but no law shall be enacted which would impair rights existing or arising by virtue of any treaty or international agreement entered into by the United States, nor shall the lands or other property of nonresidents be taxed at a higher rate than the lands or other property of residents."

---

[54] 48 U.S.C.A. § 1561.

[55] 48 U.S.C.A. § 1574.

Sec. 3. Subsection (e) of section 8 of said Act is amended by striking the words "and any supplements to it".

Sec. 4. Subsection (a) of section 17 of said Act [56] is amended by striking the words "not to exceed".

Sec. 5. Subsections (e) and (f) of section 17 of said Act are amended to read as follows:

"(e) The decisions of the government comptroller shall be final except that appeal therefrom may, with the concurrence of the Governor, be taken by the party aggrieved or the head of the Department concerned, within one year from the date of the decision, to the Secretary of the Interior, which appeal shall be in writing and shall specifically set forth the particular action of the government comptroller to which exception is taken, with the reasons and the authorities relied upon for reversing such decision.

"(f) If the Secretary of the Interior confirms the decision of the government comptroller, or if the Governor does not concur in the taking of an appeal to the Secretary, then relief may be sought by suit in the District Court of the Virgin Islands if the claim is otherwise within its jurisdiction."

Sec. 6. (a) Subsection (c) of section 20 of said Act [57] is amended to read as follows:

"(c) The salaries of the Governor, the Government Secretary, the government comptroller, and the members of their immediate staffs shall be paid by the United States. The salaries of the heads of the executive departments shall be paid by the government of the Virgin Islands; and if the legislature shall fail to make an appropriation for such salaries, the salaries theretofore fixed shall be paid without the necessity of further appropriations therefor."

(b) This section 6 shall become effective on July 1, 1959.

---

[56] 48 U.S.C.A. § 1599.

[57] 48 U.S.C.A. § 1641.

Sec. 7. The last sentence of section 24 of said Act [58] is amended to read as follows: "The Attorney General shall appoint a United States marshal for the Virgin Islands, to whose office the provisions of chapter 33 of title 28, United States Code, shall apply."

Sec. 8. The first sentence of section 26 of said Act [59] is amended to read as follows: "All criminal cases originating in the district court shall be tried by jury upon demand by the defendant or by the Government."

Sec. 9. Wherever the term "district attorney" appears in the seventh and eighth sentences of section 27 of said Act [60] the following term shall be substituted: "United States attorney".

Sec. 10. The first sentence of subsection (b) of section 8 of said Act is amended to read as follows: "The legislature of the government of the Virgin Islands may cause to be issued on behalf of said government bonds or other obligations (1) for a specific public improvement or specific public undertaking authorized by an act of the legislature, and (2) for the establishment, construction, operation, maintenance, reconstruction, improvement, or enlargement of other projects, authorized by an act of the legislature, which will, in the legislature's judgment, promote the public interest by economic development of the Virgin Islands. Such bonds or obligations shall be payable solely from the revenues directly derived from and attributable to such specific public improvement, public undertaking, or other project."

Sec. 11. As used in this Act, the term "Revised Organic Act of the Virgin Islands" means the Act of July 22, 1954 (68 Stat. 497), as amended (48 U.S.C., secs. 1541 et seq.).[61]

Approved August 28, 1958.

---

[58] 48 U.S.C.A. § 1614.

[59] 48 U.S.C.A. § 1616.

[60] 48 U.S.C.A. § 1617.

[61] 48 U.S.C.A. § 1541 et seq.

70a

APPENDIX J

(Bill 2638)

No. 1518

(Approved August 30, 1965)

To Impose Certain Production Taxes on Watches Manufactured in the Virgin Islands, and for Other Purposes.

Be it enacted by the Legislature of the Virgin Islands:

Section 1. The following new sections 511 to 518 are added to Chapter 9, Title 33 of the Virgin Islands Code:

"§ 511.(a) There shall be imposed upon watches manufactured in the Virgin Islands, when sold, or removed for sale, consumption or use, a tax at the rate of $2.50 per watch.

"(b) A credit of $2.47 per watch shall be allowed upon:

"(1) watches manufactured and sold for disposition in the course of retail trade in the Virgin Islands;

"(2) watches manufactured and exported to other than the customs area of the United States;

"(3) watches manufactured pursuant to a quota allocated to such manufacture in accordance with the provisions of sections 512 or 513 of this chapter.

"(c) For the purpose of sections 511 through 518 of this chapter, 'watches manufactured in the Virgin Islands' includes not only all watches resulting from the processing of raw materials or other component parts, whether by hand or machinery or both, but also all watches mechanical or otherwise, or assembly of watch movements with respect to which substantial industrial operations are undertaken in the Virgin Islands which, in the judgment of the

Governor of the Virgin Islands, affect the economic stability and the commercial relations of the Virgin Islands.

"(d) The manufacturer liable for the payment of tax hereunder shall in each case submit such proof as may be required by the Governor as is satisfactory to establish the rate or rates of tax applicable under subsections (a) and (b) of this section to the watch production of such manufacturer.

"(e) It shall be obligatory that the tax imposed by subsection (a) of this section be paid periodically, either by the manufacturer, an immediate or secondary purchaser from the manufacturer, or a contract or common carrier, at such intervals and in accordance with such rules and regulations as shall be adopted pursuant to this title by the Governor.

"§ 512. An amount of 1,800,000 units of watches is hereby established as the maximum amount of watch production consistent with the protection of the economic stability and commercial relations of the Virgin Islands for the period October 1, 1965, to March 31, 1966. Of this amount, the Governor is authorized to allocate 1,500,000 units among manufacturers of watches having a continuous watch manufacturing and shipping record in the Virgin Islands since October 1, 1964, in accordance with the procedure and criteria set forth in section 514 of this chapter. The remaining 300,000 units of watches are reserved as a quantity to be granted in order to relieve against severe financial hardship, and to permit allocation to new manufacturers. All units of watches allocated as quotas to manufacturers under this section shall be entitled to a $2.47 credit per watch.

"§ 513. (a) For each 12-month period subsequent to March 31, 1966, the Governor shall determine, after due investigation, the total annual consumption of watches of all kinds in the customs area of the United States and shall allocate among the manufacturers of watches in the Virgin Islands on that date in accordance with the criteria set forth in section 514(b) such number of units as shall total 1/9 of annual consumption.

"(b) Of the maximum amount of watch production determined in accordance with subsection (a) of this section, not to exceed five percent shall be reserved as a quantity to supplement quotas allocated to manufacturers and to relieve against severe financial hardship, in accordance with the provisions of section 515 of this chapter. The Governor is authorized to allocate the remainder among manufacturers of watches in the Virgin Islands in accordance with the procedure and criteria set forth in section 514 of this chapter. All units of watches allocated as quotas to manufacturers under this section shall be entitled to $2.47 credit per watch.

"§ 514. (a) Each person engaged or proposing to engage in the manufacture of watches in the Virgin Islands may apply to the Governor for an allocation of the amount of watch production entitled to the $2.47 credit. Such application shall be in writing, shall be on such forms, and shall contain such information, duly certified by independent accountants or auditors as may be required by the Governor in accordance with the provisions of sections 511 to 518 of this chapter or regulations thereunder.

"(b) Except as to such portions thereof as shall have been set aside as a reserve, the total maximum amount of watch production entitled to the $2.47 credit per watch shall be allocated for specific periods among applicants in accordance with the following criteria:

"(1) 66⅔ percent of such amount shall be apportioned among manufacturers in accordance with their respective percentages of total payroll in the Virgin Islands subject to Social Security taxation (exclusive of managerial or administrative personnel) incurred in watch manufacture;

for disposition in the course of retail trade in the Virgin Islands; for export to other than the customs area of the United States; and for watches manufactured pursuant to a quota allocation in accordance with sections 512 or 513 of this chapter; for such six month period nearest to the beginning of the period involved as the Governor may determine to be feasible.

"(2) 33⅔ percent of said amount shall be apportioned among manufacturers in proportion to the total number of watches:

> manufactured and sold for disposition in the course of retail trade in the Virgin Islands;

> exported to other than the customs area of the United States; and manufactured and shipped under quota allocation to the customs area of the United States;

> during the same six month period as provided for in (1) above.

"(c) The Governor shall have the authority to grant an application on temporary basis during such period as may be necessary to conduct and make determinations in accordance with investigations pursuant to section 513(a) or to make final disposition of application.

"(d) The Governor may upon due notice and hearing, refuse an application for an allocation or may revoke, modify or suspend an apportionment made to a manufacturer hereunder as in his judgment may be necessary to protect the economic stability and the commercial relations of the Virgin Islands upon a finding that

"(1) the manufacturer is not in good faith organized for the purpose of the manufacture of watches in the Virgin Islands; or

"(2) the application is or was made for the purpose of frustrating or defeating the purposes of this chapter in protecting the economic stability and commercial relations of the Virgin Islands; or

"(3) the manufacturer has discontinued the manufacture of watches in the Virgin Islands; except that (i) a temporary interruption of production attributable to normal business reasons shall not be deemed in itself a discontinuance of manufacture of watches within the meaning of this subparagraph, and (ii) nothing in this subparagraph shall prohibit the sale of a business to which a quota has been assigned, but no quota may be purchased or sold apart from the sale of the business;

"(4) the manufacturer has misrepresented material facts in connection with his application, or has failed or refused to submit information as required; or

"(5) the manufacturer has failed to utilize wholly or partially, the quota assigned to him.

"(e) In the apportionment of quotas to a manufacturer hereunder, the Governor is authorized to take into account, and to make a corresponding deduction, watch for watch, where such is in his judgment necessary to protect the economic stability and the commercial relations of the Virgin Islands, of any quantity of watches shipped to the customs area of the United States by the same manufacturer, or a firm corporately or personally affiliated, from any other territory or possession of the United States.

"(f) Whenever the Governor shall determine upon due notice and hearing, that all or part of a quota allocated to a manufacturer shall remain unused at the end of a quota period, he may cancel the allocation, in whole or in part, as the case may be, and such allocation, in whole or in part may be reallocated to another manufacturer or placed in the reserves provided for in section 512 or 513(b) of this chapter.

"§ 515. In making grants out of the reserve amount provided for in sections 512, and 513(b) of this chapter, the Governor shall give special weight to the maintenance and promotion of employment, and to the complete assembly of watches from individual component parts and other characteristics of production contributing special value to the Virgin Islands. The Governor shall also take into account, but is not limited to the consideration of the following factors: investment in plant and equipment for watchmaking in the Virgin Islands; minimum quantities required for production without loss, and abnormal or unforeseeable economic circumstances.

"§ 516. The Governor is authorized to designate such individuals or groups from time to time as he may deem necessary for the purpose of assisting or advising him in the performance of his duties and responsibilities, and the exercise of his authority under the provisions of sections 511 to 518 of this chapter.

"§ 517. The Governor shall have authority to issue such rules, regulations and requirements as he may deem necessary or appropriate to effectuate and implement the provisions of sections 511 to 517 of this chapter, including but not limited to the prescribing of forms and requirements of reports and the issuance of stamps or other evidence of payment of taxes.

"§ 518. Any decision or determination made by the Governor under the provisions of this chapter as to questions of fact shall be deemed final in any proceedings in any court except upon a

APPENDIX K

(Bill 2780)

No. 1631

(Approved March 22, 1966)

To Amend Certain Provisions of Chapter 9, Title 33 of the Virgin Islands Code Relating to Production Taxes on Watches Manufactured in the Virgin Islands.

Be it enacted by the Legislature of the Virgin Islands:

Section 1. Subsection (a) of section 511 of Title 33 of the Virgin Islands Code is hereby amended to read as follows:

"§ 511. (a) There shall be imposed upon watches, clocks and timing apparatus manufactured in the Virgin Islands, when sold, or removed for sale, consumption or use, a tax at the rate of $2.50 per watch, clock, or unit of timing apparatus except as provided in section 513 of this chapter.

Section 2. Subsection (b), section 511 of said Title 33 is amended to read:

"(b) For the purposes of sections 511 through 518 of this chapter, 'watches, clocks and timing apparatus manufactured in the Virgin Islands' includes not only all watches, clocks and timing apparatus resulting from the processing of raw materials or other component parts, whether by hand or machinery or both, but also all watches, clocks and timing apparatus, mechanical or otherwise, or assembly of watch or clock movements or timing apparatus with respect to which substantial industrial operations are undertaken in the Virgin Islands which, in the judgment of the Governor of the Virgin Islands, affect the economic stability and the commercial relations of the Virgin Islands."

Section 3. Section 513 of said Title 33 is amended to read as follows:

"(a) For each 12-month period subsequent to March 31, 1966, the Governor shall determine, after due investigation, the total annual consumption of watches of all kinds within the customs area of the United States and shall allocate among manufacturers of watches in the Virgin Islands during each 12-month period subsequent to March 31, 1966, in accordance with the criteria set forth in section 514(b) of this title, such number of units as shall total 1/9 of such annual consumption. The Governor is authorized to make preliminary and partial allocations, which allocations may be completed in such installments as the Governor finds reasonable and convenient.

"(b) If in any 12-month period subsequent to March 31, 1966, clocks, or timing apparatus other than watches are produced in the Virgin Islands, the Governor shall determine, after due investigation, the total annual consumption of clocks and the total annual consumption of the same or similar timing apparatus in the customs area of the United States and shall allocate among (1) Virgin Islands manufacturers of clocks and/or (2) Virgin Islands manufacturers of timing apparatus other than watches, such number of units as shall total 1/9 of such annual consumption of clocks and such number of units as shall total 1/9 of such timing apparatus other than watches. Such allocations shall be in accordance with provisions established herein with respect to watches. In the event that a manufacturer produces more than one category of products for which an allocation is to be made, his allocation for each category of product shall be separately determined and an apportionment of his payroll reported under section 514(b)(1) of this title shall be required to be made, in accordance with such rules and regulations as shall be adopted by the Governor.

"(c) Of the maximum amount of production of watches, clocks or timing apparatus determined in accordance with subsections (a) and (b) of this section not to exceed five percent in each category shall be reserved as a quantity to supplement quotas allocated to manufacturers and to relieve against severe financial hardship, in accordance with the provisions of section 515 of this chapter. The Governor is authorized to allocate the remainder among manufacturers in the Virgin Islands of watches, clocks or timing apparatus in accordance with the criteria set forth in section 514 of this chapter. In the event that a manufacturer produces more than one category of products for which an allocation is to be made, his allocation for each category of product shall be separately determined and an apportionment of his payroll reported under section 514(b)(1) of this chapter shall be required to be made in accordance with such rules and regulations as shall be adopted by the Governor.

"(d) Upon the proclamation by the Governor of determinations made pursuant to the foregoing, the rate of tax imposed by this chapter shall be 3 cents per watch, clock or unit of timing apparatus upon the amount of production for each category of product set forth in such determinations, and the rate of tax on the excess of such amount shall be $2.50 per watch, clock or unit of timing apparatus."

Section 4. Subsections (a) and (b) of section 514 of said Title 33 are amended to read as follows:

"§ 514. (a) Each person engaged or proposing to engage in the manufacture of watches, clocks or timing apparatus in the Virgin Islands may apply to the Governor for an allocation of the amount of watch, clock or timing apparatus production to be governed by the 3 cents per watch rate. Such application shall be in writing, shall be on such forms, and shall contain such information, duly certified by independent accountants or auditors as may be required by the Governor in accordance with the provisions of sections 511 to 518 of this chapter or regulations thereunder.

"(b) For all periods subsequent to March 31, 1966, the total maximum amount of watch production taxable at the 3 cents per watch rate shall be allocated for specific periods among applicants in accordance with the following criteria:

"(1) 66⅔ percent of such amount shall be apportioned among manufacturers in accordance with their respective percentage of total payroll in the Virgin Islands (exclusive of managerial or administrative personnel) incurred and attributable to watch manufacture, during such six months period nearest to the beginning of the period involved as the Governor may determine to be most feasible in the interests of the economic stability and commercial relations of the Virgin Islands, but including in such payroll a maximum amount for any person employed of $400 per month during any calendar month of 1965 and of $550 per month during the calendar year 1966 and subsequent years.

"(2) 33⅓ percent of said amount shall be apportioned among manufacturers in proportion to the total amount of watches manufactured and on which a tax at the rate of 3 cents per watch was paid during the same six-month period as provided for in (1) above."

Section 5. Subparagraphs (1) and (3) of subsection (d), section 514 of said Title 33 are amended to read as follows:

"(1) the manufacturer is not in good faith organized for the purpose of the manufacture of watches, clocks or timing apparatus in the Virgin Islands; or"

"(3) the manufacturer has discontinued the manufacture of watches, clocks or timing apparatus in the Virgin Islands; except that (i) a temporary interruption of production attributable to normal business reasons shall not be deemed in itself a discontinuance of manufacture within the meaning of this subparagraph, and (ii) nothing in this section shall prohibit the sale of a business to which a quota has been assigned, but no quota may be purchased or sold apart from the sale of the business;".

Section 6. Subsection (e), section 514 of said Title 33 is amended to read as follows:

"(e) In the apportionment of quotas to a manufacturer hereunder, the Governor is authorized to take into account, and to make a corresponding deduction, unit for unit of the category of product, where such is in his judgment necessary to protect the economic stability and the commercial relations of the Virgin Islands, of any quantity of watches, clocks or units of timing apparatus manufactured in any other territory or possession of the United States by the same manufacturer, or by a subsidiary wholly or partially owned by it, a corporation with substantially the same stockholders or officers, or any noncorporate business organization a substantial financial interest in which is held by such manufacturer, or by its officers or stockholders."

Section 7. Section 515 of said Title 33 is amended to read as follows:

"§ 515. (a) A manufacturer desirous of obtaining an allocation from the five percent reserve provided for in section 513(c) of this chapter to supplement a quota or to relieve against severe financial hardship, shall establish to the satisfaction of the Governor that the granting of such allocation is warranted and consistent with the public interests of the Virgin Islands. Application therefor shall be in writing, shall state the amount required, and shall set forth any such factors as the manufacturer may deem relevant for consideration in connection with its application, including, where pertinent to the purpose for which the allocation is requested: the maintenance and promotion of employment; the complete assembly of watches from individual component parts and other characteristics of production contributing special value to the Virgin Islands; investment in plant and equipment in the Virgin Islands; minimum quantities required for production without loss; abnormal or unforeseeable economic circumstances.

"(b) The Governor, upon consideration of the material submitted an as he shall determine to be consistent with the interests of the Virgin Islands, may grant an allocation requested under this section, in whole or in part, or may deny the application."

Section 8. This Act shall become effective upon approval by the Governor.

Approved March 22, 1966.

APPENDIX L

H. R. Report No. 1726
85th Congress, 2d Session

AMENDING THE REVISED ORGANIC ACT OF THE VIRGIN ISLANDS

May 19, 1958—Committed to the Committee of the Whole House on the State of the Union and ordered to be printed.

Mr. O'Brien of New York, from the Committee on Interior and Insular Affairs, submitted the following

Report

[To accompany H. R. 12303]

The Committee on Interior and Insular Affairs, to whom was referred the bill (H.R. 12303) to amend the Revised Organic Act of the Virgin Islands, having considered the same, report favorably thereon without amendment and recommend that the bill do pass.

The purpose of H. R. 12303, introduced by Representative Aspinall, is to amend the Revised Organic Act of the Virgin Islands (68 Stat. 497) in 10 respects in order to remove ambiguities and technical imperfections which now exist in the statute.

PREVIOUS LEGISLATIVE HISTORY

The Virgin Islands were ceded to the United States by Denmark by treaty of January 25, 1917. From 1917 to 1931, the affairs of the islands were administered by naval governors appointed by the President of the United States. On February 27, 1931, by Executive Order 5556, the islands were placed under the Department of the Interior. In 1927, United States citizenship was conferred on residents of the islands.

Organic legislation was first provided the Virgin Islands by the United States with the enactment of the Organic Act of 1936 (49 Stat. 1807). The 1936 act was thoroughly revised in 1954, in order to remedy deficiencies which had become apparent in the 1936 act and to streamline the basic governmental organization. The 1954 act also laid a base for local development of an islandwide incentive program for attraction of new industries and tourists. Minor amendments to the 1954 act were made in the act of August 30, 1957 (71 Stat. 510).

Need for the present legislation was brought out during hearings held in the Virgin Islands by the Subcommittee on Territorial and Insular Affairs in December 1956, and by subsequent requests received from officials of the Virgin Islands government, the Department of the Interior, and the United States Court of Appeals for the Third Circuit.

H. R. 12303 was drafted and introduced following committee hearings on H. R. 2127, also introduced by Representative Aspinall.

SECTIONAL ANALYSIS

Section 1 provides that no political or religious test other than an oath to support the Constitution, the laws of the United States applicable to the Virgin Islands, and the laws of the Virgin Islands itself shall be required of Territorial officeholders.

Section 2 amends section 8(a) of the existing law under which Territorial legislature's power extends "to all subjects of local application." The amendment would make this read: "to all rightful subjects of legislation." In *Granville-Smith* v. *Granville-Smith,* 349 U.S. 1 (1955), the Supreme Court held that, at least with respect to persons who are not permanent residents of the islands, the phrase "subjects of local application" has a meaning narrower than the phrase "rightful subjects of legislation." The latter language is used in the Organic Acts of Alaska and Hawaii.

Section 3 pertains to the expense of printing supplements to the Virgin Islands Code. The code has been prepared, approved by the Virgin Islands Legislature, printed at Federal expense and distributed. The committe believes that any supplements that may be prepared should be at the expense of the Virgin Islands government.

Section 4 refers to the salary of the government comptroller of the Virgin Islands which is presently set at not to exceed $12,500 per annum. The proposed amendment to the Organic Act will delete the words "not to exceed," thus permitting the comptroller to receive the 25 percent overseas pay differential which other Federal employees in the Virgin Islands enjoy.

Section 5 refers to appeals from decisions rendered by the government comptroller. It provides that his decisions shall be subject to review by Secretary of the Interior rather than the Governor, as now provided. It also provides that if the Secretary confirms the comptroller's decision, relief may be sought in appropriate cases through the District Court of the Virgin Islands.

Section 6 concerns payment of the salaries of ranking Federal officials and the heads of the executive departments in the Virgin Islands. It provides that the Federal officers and their immediate staff members shall be paid by the United States and that department heads shall be paid by the government of the Virgin Islands. It also provides that if the legislature fails to make appropriation for those salaries for which it is responsible, they shall be paid without the necessity of such appropriations. The effective date of section 6 is July 1, 1959.

Section 7 is a clarifying amendment referring to the appointment of the marshal and deputy marshal for the Virgin Islands and to the applicability of certain provisions of the United States Code to the office and officers.

Section 8 clarifies section 26 of the Revised Organic Act of the Virgin Islands which concerns the right to trial by jury in criminal cases.

Section 9 amends the section 27 of Revised Organic Act of the Virgin Islands which refers to the United States attorney for the Virgin Islands. In the seventh and eighth sentences of section 27, this official is designated as district attorney, whereas he is properly designated elsewhere in the section. This amendment will correct the existing discrepancy.

Section 10 adds a new section to the Revised Organic Act, which will expressly repeal the Organic Act of June 22, 1936. The failure of the 1954 act to repeal expressly the earlier act has created confusion as to its status. The repeal will apply in particular to section 36 of the 1936 act and will thus remove (1) the present bar against enactment by the Territorial legislature of laws concerning import duties and customs and (2) the jurisdiction of the Treasury Department over customs of the Virgin Islands. The Territorial legislature will be free, if it wishes to do so, to repeal the 6-percent duty on foreign goods imported into the Virgin Islands.

With the advent of a free port, the Virgin Islands hope to increase their tourist industry considerably and thereby to improve their economic situation. In this regard, however, the committee members take note that in fiscal year 1956 the customs receipts in the Virgin Islands were about $290,000 and the cost of customs operations was about $130,000. It also notes that the value of goods imported into the United States (including Puerto Rico) from the Virgin Islands has risen from $3,788,757 in 1954 to $3,872,010 in 1955 and to $5,210,485 in 1956.

Section 11 defines the term "Revised Organic Act of the Virgin Islands" as it is used elsewhere in H. R. 12303.

Reports Submitted

Reports were received from several departments interested in H. R. 12303 and are included as follows:

* * * * * * * * * *

DEPARTMENT OF THE TREASURY,
Washington, D. C.

Hon. CLAIR ENGLE,

Chairman, Committee on Interior and Insular Affairs,
House of Representatives, Washington, D. C.

MY DEAR MR. CHAIRMAN: The Treasury Department has noted H. R. 2127, to amend the Revised Organic Act of the Virgin Islands, and wishes to offer its views to your committee. There seem to be several possibly untoward results of which your committee should be aware and examine before coming to any conclusions regarding the proposed legislation.

The only provision of interest to the Treasury Department in H. R. 2127 is section 4, which would repeal the Organic Act of the Virgin Islands, approved June 22, 1936. The bill also would provide that the authority of the Secretary of the Treasury conferred by the second proviso in section 36 of the Organic Act would not terminate until 60 days following the date of enactment of this bill.

Section 36 of the Organic Act of the Virgin Islands is the present statutory authority of the Secretary of the Treasury to administer the customs laws applicable to the Virgin Islands. The repeal of that section as proposed by section 4 of H. R. 2127 would (1) remove the present bar against enactment by the Territorial legislature of laws concerning import duties and customs and (2) remove the jurisdiction of the Treasury Department over the customs of the Virgin Islands. The Treasury Department through the Customs Service administers the Virgin Islands tariff law as well as numerous other Federal statutes which are applicable in the islands. It is understood that one of the principal purposes of section 4 is to clear the way for repeal by the Territorial legislature of the 6-percent duty on foreign goods imported into the Virgin Islands.

The salaries and expenses for the customs operation in the Virgin Islands are paid from the duty collections there and the remainder is covered into the Territorial treasury. For fiscal year 1956 the receipts were about $290,000 and the cost of the customs operation was approximately $130,000. If the existing 6-percent duty on foreign goods imported into the Virgin Islands is eliminated, the necessity to continue to have the United States customs force there for collection of duties would disappear and the present source of funds to maintain it would be eliminated.

Without expressing any opinion on the merits of permitting repeal of the 6-percent duty on merchandise entering the Virgin Islands, the Department feels it should call the attention of your committee to section 301 of the Tariff Act of 1930, as added in 1954 (19 U.S.C. 1301a), which provides in effect for the free entry of goods coming into the United States from its insular possessions, except Puerto Rico, which do not contain foreign materials to a value of more than 50 percent (changed in 1954 from the 20 percent in effect under prior law) of their total value. It may be noted that there has been an increase in the value of goods coming into the United States from the Virgin Islands since the law was changed in 1954 from the 20 percent to the 50 percent test, as illustrated by the following tabulation:

Value of general imports into the United States (including Puerto Rico) from the Virgin Islands

Calendar year:	Total
1952	$2,477,655
1953	2,752,499
1954	3,788,757
1955	3,872,010
1956	5,210,485

The change from 20 percent to 50 percent was made at a time when the 6-percent duty was in effect for the indefinite future. Undoubtedly, removal of this duty will result in an increase in the volume of duty free importation of foreign materials into the United States, although we cannot predict the amount of the increase.

If H. R. 2127 were enacted, it would appear that there would be no provision for continued administration of certain important Federal laws which will remain applicable in the Virgin Islands. Such of those laws which are the primary concern of this Department include certain aspects of the Narcotic Control Act of 1956 and the navigation and vessel inspection laws made applicable to the islands by (1942) Executive Order 9170 (7 Fed. Reg. 384).

There are other bodies of laws applicable in the Virgin Islands which are the primary administrative responsibility of other agencies but presently enforced by the Customs Service. These laws and functions include—

(a) The gathering of trade statistics and enforcement of export-control laws for the Department of Commerce;

(b) Enforcement of Department of Agriculture laws relating to control of poisons, insect pests, packaged fruits, and wheat and wheat flour;

(c) Enforcement of Department of Health, Education, and Welfare laws relating to food, drugs, cosmetics, and certain diseased livestock;

(d) Enforcement of Department of State laws concerning arms, ammunition, and implements of war;

(e) Enforcement of Department of Justice laws relating to political propaganda; and

(f) Enforcement of laws of concern to the Atomic Energy Commission.

It is suggested that if your committee has not already done so, it may wish to obtain the views of those agencies with respect to the enforcement of such laws if H. R. 2127 were enacted.

The Treasury Department is of the opinion that the above laws can be most effectively and economically administered by its customs force owing to the long experience it has had in administering and enforcing these technical laws in the Virgin Islands and throughout the United States. If section 4 of the proposed legislation is enacted, the Secretary of the Treasury will not be concerned with the maintenance of a customs force in the Virgin Islands, and therefore there will be no established agency available to enforce these Federal laws unless other appropriate legislation is enacted.

If the Congress, as a matter of policy, determines that the present jurisdiction of the Treasury Department over the customs activities of the Virgin Islands should be discontinued, the proviso contained in section 4 of the bill would be necessary to allow for an orderly termination of the Treasury Department jurisdiction.

The Department has been advised by the Bureau of the Budget that there is no objection to the submission of this report to your committee.

Very truly yours,

DAVID W. KENDALL
Acting Secretary of the Treasury.

UNITED STATES COURT OF APPEALS
FOR THE THIRD CIRCUIT

Philadelphia, Pa., March 14, 1957.

Hon. CLAIR ENGLE,

Chairman, Committee on Interior and Insular Affairs,
House of Representatives, Washington, D. C.

DEAR CONGRESSMAN: May I submit the following comments with respect to H. R. 2127 to amend the Revised Organic Act of the Virgin Islands.

Section 1 of the bill would amend the last sentence of section 24 of the Revised Organic Act which now reads: "The Attorney General shall, as heretofore, appoint a marshal *and one deputy marshal* for the Virgin Islands to whose office the provisions of chapter 33 of title 28, United States Code, shall apply." The italicized phrase "and one deputy marshal" was inserted by amendment during the passage of the bill. The effect of its insertion in the sentence was inadvertently to render ungrammatical and ambiguous the last part of the sentence, which was intended to provide that chapter 33 should apply to the office of the marshal. The deputy marshal, being merely a subordinate in that office, of course does not have a separate independent office, but the sentence now reads as though it is to his office that chapter 33 is to apply. Section 1 of the bill corrects this error by eliminating the unnecessary reference to the deputy marshal, whose appointment is sufficiently authorized by section 542 of chapter 33 of title 28, United States Code.

Section 2 of the bill corrects another inadvertent error in the Revised Organic Act which appears in section 27. This section provides for the office of United States attorney for the Virgin Islands. This official was formerly called the district attorney. In changing the title of the office to United States attorney in section 27 the conference report inadvertently failed to make the change in the seventh and eighth sentences of the section. The result is that the title "district attorney" still appears in those two sentences and those alone. Section 2 of the bill corrects this error by substituting "United States attorney" for "district attorney" wherever the latter appears in those two sentences.

Section 3 of the bill corrects an ambiguity appearing in section 26 of the Revised Organic Act which was carried forward without correction from the Organic Act of 1936. It appears in the first sentence of section 26 which is as follows: "In any criminal case originating in the district court, no person shall be denied the right to trial by jury *on the demand of either party.*" The italicized phrase in this sentence "on the demand of either party" is extremely ambiguous and confusing. It is clear that the legislative intention was that a defendant in a criminal case in the district court should not be denied the right to a jury trial if he demands it. It is meaningless, however, to provide, as the present language in effect does, that no person shall be denied the right to trial by jury if the other party, the government, demands it. For in such a case the defendant not having himself demanded a jury trial must be assumed not to desire it and, therefore, his failure to receive it would not be a denial of a right even though the government demanded a jury trial. Section 3 of the bill removes all ambiguity in this language by making it explicit that a jury trial shall be had if demanded by either the defendant or the government.

Section 4(a) of the bill would add a new section 37 to the Revised Organic Act expressly repealing the former Organic Act of 1936. The failure of the Revised Organic Act to repeal its predecessor of 1936 was an inadvertence which has caused confusion as to the present status of the organic law of the Territory. This section would rectify this error with an appropriate interim proviso with respect to section 36 of the old act.

Section 4(b) of the bill would correct another inadvertent error in the Revised Organic Act, i.e., the omission from it of the provision of the 1936 act prohibiting the imposition of a political or religious test as to qualification for holding office under the government of the Virgin Islands. This provision should obviously be reinstated.

I believe that all of the amendments proposed by H. R. 2127 are necessary to correct obvious error and I hope that the bill may be enacted promptly.

Sincerely yours,

ALBERT B. MARIS.

The Committee on Interior and Insular Affairs recommends the enactment of H. R. 12303.

CHANGES IN EXISTING LAW

In compliance with clause 3 of rule XIII of the Rules of the House of Representatives, changes in existing law made by the bill, as introduced, are shown as follows (existing law proposed to be omitted is enclosed in black brackets, new matter is printed in italics, existing law in which no change is proposed is shown in roman):

ACT OF JULY 22, 1954 (68 Stat. 497), AS AMENDED (48 U.S.C. SECS. 1541 ET SEQ.)

AN ACT to revise the Organic Act of the Virgin Islands of the United States

Be it enacted by the Senate and House of Representatives of the United States of America in Congress assembled, That this Act may be cited as the "Revised Organic Act of the Virgin Islands".

Sec. 2. (a) The provisions of this Act, and the name "Virgin Islands" as used in this Act, shall apply to and include the territorial domain islands, bays, and waters acquired by the United States through cession of the Danish West Indian Islands by the convention between the United States of America and His Majesty the King of Denmark entered into August 4, 1916, and ratified by the Senate on September 7, 1916 (39 Stat. 1706). The Virgin Islands as above described are hereby declared an unincorporated territory of the United States of America.

(b) The government of the Virgin Islands shall have the powers set forth in this Act and shall have the right to sue by such name and in cases arising out of contract, to be sued: *Provided,* That no tort action shall be brought against the government of the Virgin Islands or against any officer or employee thereof in his official capacity without the consent of the legislature constituted by this Act.

The capital and seat of government of the Virgin Islands shall be located at the city of Charlotte Amalie, in the island of St. Thomas.

*　　*　　*　　*　　*　　*　　*　　*　　*　　*

(b) Sessions of the legislature shall be held in the capital of the Virgin Islands at Charlotte Amalie, Saint Thomas.

Sec. 8. [(a) The legislative authority and power of the Virgin Islands shall extend to all subjects of local application not inconsistent with this Act or the laws of the United States made applicable to the Virgin Islands, but no law shall be enacted which would impair rights existing or arising by virtue of any treaty or international agreement entered into by the United States, nor shall the lands or other property of nonresidents be taxed at a higher rate than the lands or other property of residents.] *(a) The legislative authority and power of the Virgin*

Islands shall extend to all rightful subjects of legislation not inconsistent with this Act or the laws of the United States made applicable to the Virgin Islands, but no law shall be enacted which would impair rights existing or arising by virtue of any treaty or international agreement entered into by the United States, nor shall the lands or other property of nonresidents be taxed at a higher rate than the lands or other property of residents.

   *   *   *   *   *   *   *   *   *

SEC. 36. If any clause, sentence, paragraph, or part of this Act, or the application thereof to any person, or circumstances, is held invalid, the application thereof to other persons, or circumstances, and the remainder of the Act, shall not be affected thereby.

SEC. 37. *The Organic Act of the Virgin Islands of the United States, approved June 22, 1936 (49 Stat. 1807), as amended, and all laws and parts of laws in conflict with this Act, except for the Act of January 28, 1956 (70 Stat. 5), are hereby repealed.*

APPENDIX M

Senate Report No. 2267, August 8, 1958

The Committee on Interior and Insular Affairs, to whom was referred the bill (H. R. 12303) to amend the Revised Organic Act of the Virgin Islands, having considered the same, report favorably thereon with amendments and recommend that the bill as amended do pass.

The purpose of H. R. 12303, as amended, is to amend the Revised Organic Act of the Virgin Islands (68 Stat. 497) in many respects in order to remove ambiguities and imperfections which now exist in the statute.

PREVIOUS LEGISLATION HISTORY

The Virgin Islands were ceded to the United States by Denmark by treaty of January 25, 1917. From 1917 to 1931, the affairs of the islands were administered by naval governors appointed by the President of the United States. On February 27, 1931, by Executive Order 5556, the islands were placed under the Department of the Interior. In 1927, United States citizenship was conferred on residents of the islands.

Organic legislation was first provided the Virgin Islands by the United States with the enactment of the Organic Act of 1936 (49 Stat. 1807). The 1936 act was thoroughly revised in 1954, in order to remedy deficiencies which had become apparent in the 1936 act and to streamline the basic governmental organization. Minor amendments to the 1954 act were made in the act of August 30, 1957 (71 Stat. 510).

Need for the present legislation was brought out by requests received from officials of the Virgin Islands government, the Department of the Interior, and the United States Court of Appeals for the Third Circuit.

Sectional Analysis

Section 1 provides that no political or religious test other than an oath to support the Constitution, the laws of the United States applicable to the Virgin Islands, and the laws of the Virgin Islands itself shall be required of Territorial officeholders.

Section 2 amends section 8(a) of the existing law under which Territorial legislature's power extends "to all subjects of local application." The amendment would make this read: "to all rightful subjects of legislation." In *Granville-Smith* v. *Granville-Smith*, 349 U.S. 1 (1955), the Supreme Court held that, at least with respect to persons who are not permanent residents of the islands, the phrase "subjects of local application" has a meaning narrower than the phrase "rightful subjects of legislation." The latter language is used in the Organic Acts of Alaska and Hawaii.

The committee is of the opinion that the term "rightful subjects of legislation" is well known in the law, and its application to the legislative power of the Territory should prevent the development of a jurisdictional no man's land where neither Federal nor Territorial law can apply. Under the language of section 2 of the bill, the legislative jurisdiction of the Territory would cover the ordinary area of sovereign legislative power as limited and circumscribed by the Revised Organic Act or the laws of the United States made applicable to the Virgin Islands. The Congress retains, of course, the power to disapprove, modify, and supersede any and all acts of the Territorial legislature.

Section 3 pertains to the expense of printing supplements to the Virgin Islands Code. The code has been prepared, approved by the Virgin Islands Legislature, printed at Federal expense and distributed. The committee believes that any supplements that may be prepared should be at the expense of the Virgin Islands government.

Section 4 refers to the salary of the government comptroller of the Virgin Islands which is presently set at not to exceed $12,500 per annum. The proposed amendment to the Organic Act will delete the words, "not to exceed," thus permitting the comptroller to receive the 25-percent overseas pay differential which other Federal employees in the Virgin Islands enjoy.

Section 5 changes the procedure for appeals from decisions of the government comptroller. The aggrieved party or department may apply to the Governor for permission to appeal to the Secretary of the Interior. If permission is not granted, relief may be sought in the District Court of the Virgin Islands. If the Governor grants permission and the Secretary confirms the decision of the government comptroller; then, also, relief may be sought in said court.

Section 6 amends the present law to provide that the government comptroller and the members of his immediate staff shall be paid by the United States instead of by the Territorial government. The committee agrees with the Department of the Interior that the government comptroller should not be dependent on appropriation action by the Territorial legislature for the funds to carry on his functions.

Section 7 is an amendment referring to the appointment of the marshal for the Virgin Islands and to the applicability of certain provisions of the United States Code to the office and officers. This section was amended by the committee to allow the appointment of more than one deputy if more are required to perform the duties of the office.

Section 8 clarifies section 26 of the Revised Organic Act of the Virgin Islands which concerns the right to trial by jury in criminal cases.

Section 9 amends the section 27 of Revised Organic Act of the Virgin Islands which refers to the United States attorney for the Virgin Islands. In the seventh and eighth sentences of section 27, this official is designated as district attorney, whereas he is properly designated elsewhere in the section. This amendment will correct the existing discrepancy.

Section 10 of the bill as it passed the House of Representatives was deleted by the committee. One of the main results of the former section would be the discontinuance of Federal control over the rates of customs duties on goods imported into the Virgin Islands. The section would also have terminated the authority of the Treasury Department to administer such customs. Such action would have resulted in an increase in the burden on the United States Treasury to support Treasury functions in the islands, such increase amounting to at least $42,000 per year. The section would likewise necessitate the reorganization of certain functions of other Federal agencies in the islands. For these reasons it was decided to strike out the section and reconsider the subject when the appropriate details have been worked out.

Section 11 of the bill as it passed the House of Representatives would have ratified a Territorial act establishing a tax-incentive program to foster economic development of the islands. The Treasury Department is unalterably opposed to section 11. A delegation from the Territorial legislature agreed to deletion of the section to prevent jeopardizing the rest of the bill and to allow time to work over the tax-incentive program along such lines as will meet with the approval of the Congress and the interested Federal agencies.

Section 10 of the bill, as reported, expands the power of the Territory to issue revenue bonds. Such bonds must be issued on behalf of the Territorial government and cannot be issued by agencies or instrumentalities thereof. The Territory can issue no general obligation bonds whatsoever.

Under the section, the legislature could authorize revenue bonds to be issued by the Territorial government to finance projects to promote economic development of the islands. Each such project would require specific approval and bond authorization to this section is to require that the legislature specifically consider and decide whether such projects for economic development are in the public interest.

Section 11 of the bill, as amended, defines the term "Revised Organic Act of the Virgin Islands" as it is used elsewhere in H. R. 12303.

UNITED STATES COURT OF APPEALS
FOR THE THIRD CIRCUIT

Philadelphia, Pa., June 20, 1958.

Hon. HENRY M. JACKSON,

Chairman, Subcommittee on Territories and Insular Affairs, Committee on Interior and Insular Affairs, United States Senate, Washington, D. C.

DEAR SENATOR JACKSON: H. R. 12303, to amend the Revised Organic Act of the Virgin Islands, passed the House on June 16 and is now, I believe, in your subcommittee. The bill makes a number of important and much-needed amendments and I would urge its early and favorable consideration. My specific comments with respect to certain of the amendments proposed by the bill and the need for them are set out in detail in a letter to Chairman Engle of the House Committee on Interior and Insular Affairs which appears in the House committee report (H. Rept. No. 1726, 85th Cong., 2d sess.) at pages 11 and 12, and need not be repeated here. My purpose in writing you at this time is to suggest a change which my experience as acting judge of the district court of the Virgin Islands since the retirement of Judge Moore indicates to me is needed in one of the amendments proposed by the bill, because of changes brought about by the Virgin Islands Code.

I refer to section 7 of the bill which would amend the last sentence of section 24 of the Revised Organic Act so as to straighten out the present ambiguous language with respect to the marshal for the Virgin Islands. Prior to September 1, 1957, the duties of the marshal did not include the service of summonses and writs or the levy upon, attachment or sale of real and personal property upon execution writs. All these duties were the performed by the chief of police and his force. The revised organic act accordingly stipulated that the marshal should have only one deputy and that was undoubtedly all the assistance he then needed.

However, by the Virgin Islands Code, title 4, section 38, which went into effect on September 1, 1957, it was made the duty of the marshal to execute all writs, process, and orders of the district court, a duty which all other United States marshals have performed from time immemorial. The result is that the marshal now has a substantial volume of business coming to him currently. And since the court operates in two judicial divisions, the division of St. Thomas and St. John, and the division of St. Croix, the marshal must now maintain offices for the accommodation of the court and the bar in both St. Thomas and St. Croix. Under these new circumstances he may well need two deputies, one permanently stationed in St. Thomas and the other permanently stationed in St. Croix, in view of the 40 miles of ocean which separate the two islands and the difficulty and expense of travel between them.

I would accordingly suggest that the limiting words "and one deputy marshal" be stricken from the amendment of section 24 of the revised organic act which is proposed to be made by section 7 of H. R. 12303. These words are not necessary to authorize the appointment of a deputy since the Attorney General now has that power under section 543 of chapter 33 of title 28, United States Code, and if the words are stricken out the Attorney General would be left free to determine in accordance with the needs of the service the number of deputies to be appointed from time to time by the marshal in the Virgin Islands, just as he now does in the case of all other marshals including the marshals in Alaska, the Canal Zone, Guam, Hawaii, and Puerto Rico. Thus it would make it possible for the Attorney General to authorize the appointment of a deputy in each of the two judicial divisions of the Virgin Islands if he finds this to be necessary, as I believe he will, in order to carry on the work of the district court efficiently and expeditiously.

I hope the foregoing suggestion will be helpful to your committee.

With kindest regards, I am

Sincerely yours,

ALBERT B. MARIS.

The Committee on Interior and Insular Affairs recommends the enactment of H. R. 12303, as amended.

IN THE

Supreme Court of the United States

OCTOBER TERM 1968

MASTER TIME COMPANY, LTD.,
a Virgin Islands Corporation,
Petitioner,

v.

THE HONORABLE PERCY DEJONGH, etc.,
Respondents,

No. 1082

and

VIRGO CORPORATION,
a Virgin Islands Corporation,
Petitioner,

v.

RALPH M. PAIEWONSKY, Governor of
the Virgin Islands, et al.,
Respondents.

No. 1163

BRIEF IN OPPOSITION TO PETITIONS FOR WRITS OF CERTIORARI TO THE UNITED STATES COURT OF APPEALS FOR THE THIRD CIRCUIT

FRANCISCO CORNEIRO
*Attorney General of the
Virgin Islands*
Department of Law
P. O. Box 280
St. Thomas, Virgin Islands 00801

Of Counsel:
BRUCE MacGIBBON
Assistant Attorney General

INDEX

TABLE OF CITATIONS

Cases

PAGE

Statutes Involved

Opinions Below

The opinion of the Court of Appeals in both cases was consolidated in one opinion and reported at 384 F. 2d 569 (1967). The opinions of the District Court are reported at 5 V.I. 342, 251 F. Supp. 279; 5 V.I. 359, 254 F. Supp. 405, and 5 V.I. 417, 259 F. Supp. 26.

Questions Presented

1. Whether the legislative powers of the Virgin Islands may provide for taxation upon the manufacture of watches though the bulk of such manufactured watches are shipped to the United States.

2. Whether the Government of the Virgin Islands may deny tax exemption to an applicant on the statutory criterion of need.

Statutes Involved

The statutes involved in consideration of the first question raised by the Petitions are as follows:

Section 36 of the Organic Act of the Virgin Islands —June 22, 1936, Ch. 699, Sec. 36, 49 Stat. 1816 (MT 66a)*

August 28, 1958—Amendment to Revised Organic Act of the Virgin Islands. Public Law 85—851; 72 Stat. 1094 [H.R. 12303]; (M.T. 67a)

Act No. 1518, approved August 30, 1965 (V. I. Sess. L. 1965, p. 470)

---

* "MT" refers to the Appendix attached to the Master Time Company Brief; "V" refers to the Appendix attached to the Virgo Corporation Brief.

Act No. 1631, approved March 22, 1966 (V. I. Sess. L. 1966, p. 98)

The statutes involved in consideration of the second question, raised only by the petitioner Virgo Corporation, are contained in 33 V.I.C. sec. 4001 et seq., which pertinent portions are contained in the Appendix to the Petition of Virgo Corporation (V 78a-86a).

Statement

Respondent adopts as its Statement of Facts material to the consideration of the questions here presented the summary of the facts contained in the Opinion of the Court of Appeals.

REASONS FOR DENYING THE WRITS

I. The Court of Appeals has correctly decided that the Legislature has the authority to enact a statute which levies a tax on the manufacture of watches and that such tax is not in violation of the Commerce Clause of the Constitution nor is it a tax upon exports.

The appellants in both cases contend that the Watch Production Quota Tax (imposed by Acts Nos. 1581 and 1631) is either a tax upon exports forbidden by the Constitution and by the Organic Act of the Virgin Islands of 1936 (MT 66a), or in the alternative, in violation of the Commerce Clause of the Constitution.

The fallacy of this reasoning is that both appellants are unwilling to categorize "shipments to the United States" as exports, or in the alternative, as commerce between the States (or between States and Territories likened to States so as to bring into force the application of the Commerce Clause). These "shipments" must be for purposes of Constitutional inquiry, either

    (a) exports; or

    (b) commerce between States (or States and Territories likened to States). They must fit into some singular category.

The Government of the Virgin Islands contends that in full accord with precedents established by this Court, shipments from the Virgin Islands to the Continental United States are not exports. With the extension of its legislative authority and power, the Virgin Islands may be considered to have acquired some of the attributes of a state; nevertheless, it remains "an unincorporated territory of the United States" under the Revised Organic Act of 1954, 68 Stat. 497, sec. 2, 48 U.S.C.A., sec. 1541(a). Since it is not a state, it, like Puerto Rico, does not suffer the constitutional impediments applicable to a state. "The constitutional prohibition upon the imposition of duties or imposts on imports [or exports] is inapplicable because that prohibition is laid upon the states, and Puerto Rico, as we frequently have occasion to say, is not a state but an organized territory not incorporated into the United States." *Buscaglia* v. *Ballester*, 162 F. 2d 805, 807 (1st Cir., 1947), cert. den. 332 U.S. 816. Conversely, unlike the Phillippine Islands before it was given in many respects the status of an independent government, the Virgin Islands is not to be regarded as foreign territory. *Cf. Barber* v. *Gonzales*, 347 U.S. 637, 642, 98 L. ed. 1009, 1013 (1954); *Hoover & Allison Co.* v. *Evatt*, 324 U.S.

652, 677, 89 L. ed. 1252, 1270 (1945). ''The words 'imports' and 'exports' as therein used [Art. I, Sec. 10, U.S. Const.], have been held to apply only to articles imported from, or exported to, foreign countries.'' *Patapsco Guano Company* v. *North Carolina Board of Agriculture,* 171 U.S .345, 350, 43 L. ed. 191, 193 (1898). Thus the shipment from the Virgin Islands to the United States is neither an export nor an import under the prohibition on state import and export duties.

Thus it is contended that shipments from the Virgin Islands to the continental United States fall within the realm of *commerce,* not exports. But even in this area, assuming the regulation of such ''commerce'' by the Virgin Islands Legislature, it is contended that there are no constitutional impediments. The impediments of regulating commerce runs against states or territories which have achieved certain attributes of states, not against ''unincorporated territories.

No section of the Revised Organic Act of the Virgin Islands, or of any other law of Congress, states that the Constitution is extended to the Virgin Islands, whereas both the Organic Acts of Hawaii (48 U.S.C.A. sec. 495, 47 Stat. 205) and Alaska (48 U.S.C.A. sec. 23, 37 Stat. 512) specifically provided that the Constitution was extended to those states when they were territories. Indeed, it is well settled that except for certain provisions which guarantee or secure certain fundamental personal rights, or which limit the exercise of executive and legislative power when enacted for and over the insular possessions, the Constitution does not follow the flag into unincorporated territories. *Balzac* v. *People of Puerto Rico,* 258 U.S. 298, 66 L. ed. 627 (1922). The Congress, in the Revised Organic Act of the Virgin Islands included a "Bill of Rights" which covers substantially every one of the guaranties of the Federal Constitution. A similar provision in the Organic Act of Puerto Rico (39 Stat. at L. 951, chap. 145, known as the "Jones Act") was held by the Supreme Court in the *Balzac* case to be a conclusive argument against the contention that the Constitutional guaranties applied *ex propio vigore* to Puerto Rico.

Because the Virgin Islands is not a state but a territory, the legislative power of the Congress, and its authority to delegate that power to the territorial government, is derived from the constitutional grant of plenary control over territories, without restriction by the Commerce Clause. "Since its power . . . as to a territory like Puerto Rico is plenary except as limited by express constitutional restrictions, Congress is not fettered by the commerce clause, Const. Art. I, Sec. 8, Cl. 3, in its power to legislate for Puerto Rico." *Cases* v. *United States,* 131 F. 2d 916, 923 (1st Cir., 1942), cert. den. 319 U.S. 770 (1943), reh. den. 324 U.S. 889 (1945). Similarly, the Congress is not limited by the commerce clause in the extent to which it may delegate its legislative authority:

> "The commerce clause gives Congress plenary power to regulate our foreign and interstate commerce and thus as a necessary consequence it has the secondary effect of a restriction upon the power of the states in the premises. It thus has two aspects, but in neither of them, either as a grant of federal power or as a necessarily consequential

limitation upon state power, does it affect Puerto Rico. In its aspects of a grant of power to the federal government it adds nothing to the comprehensive power given to Congress by the Constitution, Art. IV, section 3, cl. 2, to legislative with respect to national territory, and it can have no consequential effect of limiting territorial action since Congress already has the power under Art. IV, section 3, cl. 2, supra, to limit such action to any extent it chooses, even to the extent of annulling local legislation ..."

"The actual question presented as we see it is whether Congress, in the exercise of its Constitutional power under Art. IV, section 3, cl. 2, to 'make all needful Rules and Regulations' respecting the Territory of Puerto Rico, has seen fit to give the insular government power to impose the disputed tax." *Buscaglia* v. *Ballester,* supra, 162 F. 2d at 806-807.

Although it has been held "that commerce between the States and a Territory which has become a part of the United States is interstate commerce," *Anderson* v. *Mullaney,* 191 F. 2d 123, 127 (9th Cir., 1951), affirmed at 342 U.S. 415 (1952) (Alaska), *Inter-Island Steam Nav. Co.* v. *Territory of Hawaii,* 96 F. 2d 412, 416-417 (9th Cir., 1938) (Hawaii), the Commerce Clause has been declared not to extend to an unincorporated territory, *Sancho* v. *Bacardi Corporation of America,* 109, F. 2d 57, 62-63 (1st Cir., 1940), reversed on other grounds sub nom. *Bacardi Corporation of America* v. *Domenech,* 311 U.S. 150, 95 L. ed. 98 (1940):

"... The commerce clause (U.S.C.A. Constitution, Article I, Section 8, clause 3) grants the Congress power 'To regulate Commerce with foreign nations, and among the several States, and with the Indian Tribes.' By necessary implication, it prevents a state from regulating such commerce. But Puerto Rico is not a state. It is an organized Territory of the United States, though not yet 'incorporated' into the Union, . . . and the indubitable right of the Congress to regulate the Commerce of Puerto Rico is founded on the Constitutional power 'to dispose of and make all needful Rules and Regulations respecting the Territory or other property belonging to the United States.' (Constitution, Article IV, Section 3, Clause 2). The power is in no direct sense dependent upon the Commerce Clause which as this Court has said 'does not extend to Puerto Rico.' *Lugo* v. *Suazo,* 1 Cir. 59 F. 2d 386, 390. Cf. *Inter-Island Steam Navigation Co.* v. *Hawaii,* 9 Cir., 96 F. 2d 412.

"The decree of the District Court declaring such legislation unconstitutional cannot be affirmed upon the ground that the Puerto Rican statutes violate the commerce clause of the Constitution of the United States."

Heavy emphasis was placed in the Virgo Petition on *Mullaney* v. *Anderson,* 342 U.S. 415, 96 L. ed. 1328 (1952) and by both Petitions on *Granville-Smith* v. *Granville-Smith,* 349 U.S. 1, 99 L. ed 773 (1955).

Both appellants cite these cases as indications that the Commerce Clause applies to the Territory of the Virgin Islands. A clear reading of the *Mullaney* case indicates a different conclusion. Justice Frankfurter stated in his decision that the only reasons that the Supreme Court determined that the Territory of Alaska was governed by the Commerce Clause were (1) the Alaskan Organic Act itself which states, "*the Constitution of the United States* and all laws thereof which are not locally inapplicable which have the same force and effect within the Territory as elsewhere in the United States" and (2) further, that Section 9 of the Organic Act of Alaska extended the legislative power of the territory to "all rightful subjects of legislation not inconsistent with the *Constitution* and the laws of the United States." Justice Frankfurter emphasized this by stating "*in the light of these sections* we cannot presume that Congress authorized the territorial legislature to treat citizens of states the way states cannot treat citizens of sister states." p. 420 (emphasis supplied). The District Court of Guam in 1962 noted this distinction in reference to the *Mullaney* case wherein on page 937 of *Ambrose Incorporated* v. *Maddox*, 203 F. Supp. 934 (1962), the Court states "as the Court of Appeals pointed out in the *Mullaney* case, the Congress might confer upon the territory the power to impose burdens upon commerce. This Court cannot hold that it has not done so by its approval implicit in its failure to annul."[1]

By amendment of August 28, 1958 (V 75a), Congress amended subsection (a) of Section 8 of the Revised Organic Act of the Virgin Islands to read as follows:

"(a) The legislative authority and power of the Virgin Islands is extended to all rightful subjects

---

[1] 48 U. S. C. Sec. 1574 Subparagraph (c) provides that the Legislature shall have power to enact new laws not inconsistent with any law of the United States applicable to the Virgin Islands, subject to the power of Congress to annul any such act of the Legislature.

of legislation not inconsistent with this act or the laws of the United States made applicable to the Virgin Islands but no law shall be enacted which would impair rights existing or arising by vitrue of any treaty or international agreement entered into by the United States . . .''

Conspicuously absent from this amendment is the reference that appeared in the Organic Act of Alaska that no law shall be enacted in contravention of the Constitution of the United States. This section was enacted after the case of *Granville-Smith* v. *Granville-Smith,* supra, which held that the Legislature of the Virgin Islands is limited to acts of *local application* and extended the power of the Legislature of the Virgin Islands to all *rightful subjects of legislation.* Implicit in this act is the proposition that rightful subjects of legislation are *all* subjects of legislation that a sovereign may exercise subject only to the limitations which are contained in the Organic Act; for example, in the Organic Act of Alaska, where the limitation was that legislation may not be in contravention of the Constitution of the United States. It thus seems clear that Congress in the exercise of its plenary power over the Territory of the Virgin Islands may designate a different requirement than that which it designated for a different territory, especially when Congress reserved the right to annul such legislation when it is not considered in the best interest of the United States.

Furthermore, even if the Commerce Clause, the Export-Import Clause, or the prohibition on new exports as contained in the Organic Act of 1936 could be said to be applicable in general terms to acts of the

Territorial Legislature it would not reach the imposition of production taxes on the manufacture of watches as is here complained, because the taxes are imposed on products which have not reached the stream of commerce. The test of whether the goods have ceased to be a part of the general mass of property in a state subject as such to its jurisdiction by actual entry into the stream of commerce is equally applicable under the Commerce Clause and under the Export-Import Clause. *Empresa Siderugica, S.A.* v. *County of Merced,* 337 U.S. 154, 93 L. ed. 1277 (1949).

Petitioners in both cases rely on *American Oil Company* v. *Neill,* 380 U.S. 451 (1965) for the proposition "that when passing on the constitutionality of a state taxing scheme it is firmly established that this Court concerns itself with the practical operation of its tax, that is, substance rather than form." However, what neither petitioner states is what immediately follows that quotation, which is: This approach requires us to determine the ultimate effect of the law as applied and enforced by a state or, in other words, to find *the operating incidence of the tax"* (emphasis supplied). (Ibid) It is to be noted that the facts of the *American Oil Company* case involved whether a state could tax a transaction outside of the state though there exists minimal contacts within the state itself. The Court stated that one of the outstanding prerequisites on state power to tax is the requirement that there must be "some definite link, some minimum connection between a state and the person, property or transaction it seeks to tax." (Ibid) In the Virgin Islands there is more than a minimum connection. The entire manufacturing process which the territory is taxing occurs within the territorial limits itself and the territory imposes the tax upon the sale or removal of the watches from the factory. Compare *General Motors Corporation* v. *Washington,* 377 U.S. 436, 12 L. ed. 2d 430 (1964). Furthermore, in *General Motors,* supra, the Supreme Court has stated when concerned with state taxing statutes which impinge upon Commerce, "a careful analysis of the cases in this field teaches that the validity of the tax rests upon whether the state is exacting a constitutionally fair demand for that aspect of interstate commerce to which it bears a special relation. For our purposes the decisive issue turns on the operating incidence of a tax. In other words, the question is whether the state has asserted its power in proper proportion to appellant's activities within the state and to appellant's consequent enjoinment of the opportunities and protection which the state has afforded." Id. at 440, 441. In considering the operating incidence of a tax on a purely mechanical basis, this Court has stated that the test of whether goods have ceased to be a part of the general mass of property in a state subject as such to its jurisdiction, by actual entry into the stream of commerce, is equally applicable under the Commerce Clause and under the Export-Import Clause. *Empresa Siderugica, S.A.* v. *County of Merced,* supra. "If the interstate movement has not begun, the mere fact that such a movement is contemplated does not withdraw the property from the state's power to tax it." *Minnesota* v. *Blasius,* 290 U.S. 1, 9, 78 L. ed. 131, 135 (1933).

The Virgin Islands Watch Production Quota Act in its original form and as amended was intended to be a tax on the manufacture of watches and for the collateral purpose of preventing an excess amount of watches from being so manufactured that their likely entry subsequently into the stream of commerce between the United States and the Virgin Islands would lead to a reduction in tariff advantages that the Virgin Islands currently enjoyed and which tariff advantages were a primary force in securing manufacturing endeavors in the Virgin Islands. The mere fact that this tax measure which produced revenue for the Virgin Islands also served as a deterrent to manufacture of watches in excess of a quota, which quota was reasonably believed to be that amount of watches which could safely enter the United States without provoking Congressional action to remove these tariff advantages is neither an abuse of the proper taxing authority of the Legislature of the Virgin Islands nor a matter that the Courts should concern themselves with. As stated by this Court, "It is beyond serious question that a tax does not cease to be valid merely because it regulates, discourages or even definitely deters the activities taxed." *United States* v. *Sanchez,* 340 U.S. 44, 95 L. ed. 49 (1950). See also *A. Magnano Company* v. *Hamilton,* 292 U.S. 40, 78 L. ed. 1109 and *United States* v. *Kahriger,* 345 U.S. 22, 97 L. ed. 755 (1953). Though the quota is measured by a percentage of annual consumption of watches in the United States, the quota itself is a fast figure. The measure of a quota, the same as the measure of a tax, is not the taxable event, that is to say, the operating incidence of the tax. *American Manufacturing Company* v. *St. Louis,*

250 U.S. 459, 63 L. ed. 1084. *Alaska* v. *Arctic Maid,* 366 U.S. 199, 6 L. ed. 2d 227 (1961). In *Alaska* v. *Arctic Maid,* supra, a tax was sustained though measured on the value of items which may have entered the stream of commerce. The Court states, "that, however, is the measure of the tax, not the taxable event. The taxable event is prosecuting the business of freezer ships and other floating cold storage. Part of the business is, of course, transporting frozen fish interstate. . ." In the Virgo Petition the appellant cites the cases of *Mandeville Farms* v. *American C.S.,* 334 U.S. 219, 230, 92 L. ed. 1328 (1948) and *United States* v. *Woman Sportswear Association,* 336 U.S. 460, 464 (1949), to the effect that these cases have "outmoded" the concept of interstate commerce, that commerce follows after manufacture and is not a part of it. These citations to this effect do not take into consideration *Empresa Siderugica, S.A.* v. *County of Merced,* supra, where it was stated that actual entry into the stream of commerce is the point at which either the Commerce or the Export-Import Clause applies. Furthermore, *Mandeville,* supra, is not a case concerning limitation of a state's power to tax but instead concerns an extension of the power of Congress to reach beyond traditional concepts of commerce so as to uphold the validity of Congressional action in the area of restraints of trade and monopolies, and the applicability of the Sherman Act. Likewise *United States* v. *Woman's Sportswear Association,* supra, is devoted to the same thesis, not the lack of the power of the states to legislate, but the extension of Congressional legislation in areas now considered to be within the realm of Congressional authority.

In the Master Time Petition it was contended that the cases of *A.G. Spaulding Bros. v. Edwards,* 262 U.S. 66; 67 L. ed. 865 (1923) and *Richfield Oil Corp. v. State Board of Equalization,* 329 U.S. 69; 91 L. ed. 92 (1946) hold, contrary to the case cited by the Court of Appeals, *Canton Railroad Co. v. Rogan,* 340 U.S. 511, 95 L. ed. 488 (1951), that *sale or removal* of goods is a portion of the export process. At the outset it must be remembered that these cases, unlike the instant case, involved a particular set of facts in the *application* of state laws, not the validity of the laws themselves. Here the District Court, on summary judgment in a declaratory proceeding, held that the Watch Production Quota Act, itself was invalid regardless of its application to any individual set of facts by holding that its *purpose* was to tax exports. It is this decision, based upon a void of facts as to the application of the statute, which the Court of Appeals reversed. Furthermore, it was neither the contacts of *sale* or *removal* of goods which this Court found in the *Richfield* or *Spaulding* cases to be contacts at which the operating incidence of the tax in these cases imposed a burden upon exports in contravention to the Constitution, but instead it was the contact of delivery that controlled these decisions. "The fact that *delivery to a common carrier* gave the sale immunity in *A.G. Spaulding and Bros. v. Edwards,* 262 U.S. 66, 67 L. ed. 865, 43 S. Ct. 485, supra, is seized upon as stating a rule that the process of exportation has not started until such delivery is made—" *Richfield Oil Corp. v. State Board of Equalization,* supra. The contact of "delivery" of oil into the hold of the vessel of a foreign purchaser in *Richfield Oil Corp. v. State Board of*

Equalization, supra, was the same contact which the Court in *Spaulding,* supra, seized upon to hold the application of that tax invalid as a tax on exports. The Virgin Islands imposes the Watch Production Quota Act tax on the sale or removal of goods, regardless of future deliveries, thus this is a tax wholly on manufacture, not export, unless some factual application of the tax could in a particular case show it to be a tax on exports. Nothing of this nature was before the District Court when it determined the entire format of the Watch Production Quota tax was illegal merely because that Court perceived an ulterior collateral purpose behind the tax.

II. The Governor was authorized by statute to deny Virgo's application for tax benefits on the ground that Virgo had failed to meet the requirement of need for governmental assistance.

The second question to which this brief applies is contained only in the Petition of Virgo, that is, whether the application of Virgo Corp. for tax benefits was denied improperly by the Government of the Virgin Islands "as part of an overall plan to avoid a conflict with the watch industry on the mainland" (Petition for Writ of Certiorari by Virgo Corporation, p. 19). No further reply need be given to this contention than that contained in the opinion of the Court of Appeals:

"The short answer to this contention is that the Governor stated in writing the reasons for this action, *which adequately supported it* (emphasis supplied) and political considerations were not among them. We cannot look into the Governor's mental processes nor speculate as to what they were." (V-28a)

The adequate reasons were simply that Virgo did not show that it had met the statutory requirement that it had "need" for the benefits requested; 33 V.I.C. 4001 et seq., nor did Virgo at any point in this action attempt to show that it had such need.

Conclusion

For the reasons stated, both Petitions for Writs of Certiorari should be denied.

Respectfully submitted,

FRANCISCO CORNEIRO
Attorney General of the
Virgin Islands
Department of Law
St. Thomas, Virgin Islands

Of Counsel:
BRUCE MAC GIBBON
Assistant Attorney General

CPSIA information can be obtained at www.ICGtesting.com
Printed in the USA
BVOW02s1008201214

379976BV00017B/299/P

9 781270 521365